COVENANT • BIBLE • STUDIES

Many Cultures
One in Christ

Julie Garber, Editor

faithQuest

the trade imprint of Brethren Press

Unless otherwise noted, scripture quotations are from the New Revised Standard Version of the Bible, copyrighted 1989 by the National Council of Churches
of Christ in the USA, Division of Education and Ministry.

Cover design by Jeane Healy
Cover photo © 1992 Guido Alberto Rossi / The Image Bank

96   95   94   93   92   5   4   3   2   1

Library of Congress Cataloging-in-Publication Data

Many cultures, one in Christ / Julie Garber, editor.
         p. cm. — (Covenant Bible study series)
       ISBN 0-87178-547-1
       1. Bible—Study and teaching. 2. Ethnicity—Religious
aspects—Christianity—Study and teaching. 3. Race relations—Religious
aspects—Christianity—Study and teaching. I. Garber, Julie, 1956-
II. Series.
BS600.2.M18 1992
261.8'348—dc20   92-43594
                                         CIP

Manufactured in the United States of America

Contents

Foreword

The Covenant Bible Study Series was first developed for a denominational program in the Church of the Brethren and the Christian Church (Disciples of Christ). This program, called People of the Covenant, was founded on the concept of relational Bible study and has been adopted by several other denominations and small groups who want to study the Bible in a community rather than alone.

Relational Bible study is marked by certain characteristics, some of which differ from other types of Bible study. For one, it is intended for small groups of people who can meet face-to-face on a regular basis and share frankly with an intimate group.

It is important to remember that relational Bible study is anchored in covenantal history. God covenanted with people in Old Testament history, established a new covenant in Jesus Christ, and covenants with the church today.

Relational Bible study takes seriously a corporate faith. As each person contributes to study, prayer, and work, the group becomes the real body of Christ. Each one's contribution is needed and important. "For just as the body is one and has many members, and all the members of the body, though many, are one body, so it is with Christ. . . . Now you are the body of Christ and individually members of it" (1 Cor. 12:12, 17).

Relational Bible study helps both individuals and the group to claim the promise of the Spirit and the working of the Spirit. As one person testified, "In our commitment to one another and in our sharing, something happened. . . . We were woven together in love by the master Weaver. It is something that can happen only when two or three or seven are gathered in God's name, and we know the promise of God's presence in our lives."

The symbol for these covenant Bible study groups is the burlap cross. The interwoven threads, the uniqueness of each strand, the unrefined fabric, and the rough texture characterize covenant groups. The people in the groups are unique but interrelated; they are imperfect and unpolished, but loving and supportive.

The shape that these divergent threads create is the cross, the symbol for all Christians of the resurrection and presence with us of Christ our Savior. Like the burlap cross, we are brought together, simple and ordinary, to be sent out again in all directions to be in the world.

For people who choose to use this study in a small group, the following guidelines will help create an atmosphere in which support will grow and faith will deepen.

1. As a small group of learners, we gather around God's word to discern its meaning for today.
2. The words, stories, and admonitions we find in scripture come alive for today, challenging and renewing us.
3. All people are learners and all are leaders.
4. Each person will contribute to the study, sharing the meaning found in the scripture and helping to bring meaning to others.
5. We recognize each other's vulnerability as we share out of our own experience, and in sharing we learn to trust others and to be trustworthy.

Additional suggestions for study and group-building are provided in the "Sharing and Prayer" section. They are intended for use in the hour preceding the Bible study to foster intimacy in the Covenant group and relate personal sharing to the Bible study topic.

Welcome to this study. As you search the scriptures, may you also search yourself. May God's voice and guidance and the love and encouragement of brothers and sisters in Christ challenge you to live more fully the abundant life God promises.

Preface

The preschoolers in the church nursery brought a little offering each week and put it in a small bank shaped like a church. One Sunday a child set his jaw and worked with all his might to pry open the hand of one of his classmates. There was a dull gray nickel for the offering in the girl's tightly clenched fist. When the teacher asked why they were fighting, the boy blurted out that he wanted the nickel because it was bigger than his paltry little dime!

Prizing something because of its size is typical in our society. Size affects the value of almost everything (property, business, education, even religion with its multi-million dollar enterprise churches) and determines what is the "norm." The largest culture in America, European-Americans, has set the standard of culture since coming to this country, populating the east coast and pushing its way inland and over the continent. But today, other cultures are growing and will eventually eclipse the dominant European-American culture so that it will no longer be clear whose cultural practices, if anyone's, will be the norm.

Just as the dime is smaller but more valuable than the nickel, a small culture is as rich or richer than a large one. But in our changing world, how do we know which is the best culture, which are the proper customs and traditions? This study looks to the Bible to understand how Christians should live together as a society of many cultures and races. The powerful message of Scripture tells us that God does not intend for us to blend together in a melting pot, nor stay together with "our own kind." Passages from the Old and New Testaments uphold the beauty of all cultures and use the traditions of each to increase the variety of praise we can offer to God.

Eight writers contributed to this look at multiculturalism in the church. They are Hispanic, African-, Korean-, and European-Americans. They are men and women, educators, pastors, students, writers, and church workers. Some speak authoritatively about the pain of discrimination in the church. Others confess their complicity in racism and prejudice. The writers talk about what it is like to be an outsider, whether to preserve or risk their particular religious identity, how to break down cultural barriers between people, and how to manage diversity in the church. Each offers insight into the biblical vision for cultures and challenges the church to embrace variety and the practices of other cultures.

From the covenant at Shechem to the Pentecost in the first century to today, God leads a people of infinite variety. May we be led through this study to see ourselves anew as a people of the Pentecost who do not always speak the same language or share the same cultural traditions, but who, in all our uniqueness, make up the one family of God.

THE CONTRIBUTORS

LaTaunya M. Bynum is a Senior Associate in the Center for Leadership and Ministry, Division of Homeland Ministries in the Christian Church (Disciples of Christ). Her program responsibilities include clergywomen and clergy development. She is a member of the National Council of Churches of Christ in the USA. LaTaunya earned her Master of Divinity and Doctor of Ministry degrees from the School of Theology at Claremont, California.

Julie Garber is Editor of Brethren Press, Elgin, Illinois. She is a former member of the board of the Fellowship of Reconciliation, an international peace and justice organization, and has done development work with rural communities in Nicaragua. Julie has masters degrees in theology from Bethany Theological Seminary and the University of Chicago.

Phillip E. Hoyle is Associate Minister with Monte Vista Christian Church in Albuquerque, New Mexico, and serves as the Christian Education chairperson for the Tres Rios Area of the Christian Church (Disciples of Christ) in the southwest. As chair, he has worked to establish the People of the Covenant program among area churches.

Charles Kwon is a member of Reba Place Church in Evanston, Illinois. He is on the church staff for Community and Economic Development. A graduate of M.I.T. and Northwestern's Kellogg Graduate School of Management, he is currently serving on the Korean Advisory Committee and the Young Adult Steering Committee of the Church of the Brethren.

Donald E. Miller is General Secretary of the Church of the Brethren in Elgin, Illinois, and serves on the Central Committee of the World

Council of Churches and on the Executive Coordinating Committee and the General Board of the National Council of Churches of Christ in the USA. Don earned his doctorate from Harvard University and holds degrees from the University of Chicago and Bethany Theological Seminary where he was Director of Graduate Studies and Brightbill Professor of Ministry Studies.

Frank Ramirez is a resident of Elkhart, Indiana. As a free-lance writer, he has published devotionals, articles, short stories, poems, and a novel, *The Third Letter*. He is pastor of the Elkhart Valley Church of the Brethren in Indiana.

Stephen Breck Reid was raised in the Lower Miami Church of the Brethren in Southern Ohio. He graduated from Manchester College and Bethany Theological Seminary before obtaining a doctoral degree from Emory University. He has taught in Atlanta, Berkeley, and now Austin, Texas, where he is a member of the Waka Church of the Brethren.

Olga Serrano was born in Quito, Ecuador, South America. She is a graduate of Bethany Theological Seminary and is an ordained minister. Olga organized the Church of the Brethren in Rio Prieto, Puerto Rico. Among her many projects, she works with Hispanic women and is president of the Hispanic Caucus. She now works as a teacher aide to students with emotional disorders in Santa Ana, California, where she is co-pastor of a new church project.

Related Resources

A World at Prayer: The New Ecumenical Prayer Cycle, compiled by John Carden and the World Council of Churches, offers a 52-week cycle of prayers from around the world, as well as maps and historical information on each country.

[© 1990 by Twenty-Third Publications, 185 Willow Street, P.O. Box 180, Mystic, CT 06355 (800-321-0411). 368 pages, $14.95. Available also from Brethren Press, Elgin, IL 60120 (1-800-441-3712).]

Travelling Light, by William B. McClain, presents a history of racial and ethnic exclusion and oppression in North America, challenges Christians to drop the heaviness of discrimination and "travel light," and provides reflection/discussion questions with each chapter.

[© 1981 by Friendship Press, P.O. Box 37844, Cincinnati, OH 45237. 140 pages, $3.75. Available from Brethren Press, Elgin, IL 60120 (1-800-441-3712).]

America's Original Sin: A Study Guide on White Racism, a nine-session study for adult groups, includes articles on racism and the vision for healing/reconciliation found in the gospel and discussion/action suggestions for each session.

[© 1992 by Sojourners. Available from Sojourners Resource Center, Box 29272, Washington, DC 20017 (202-636-3637). 178 pages, $10 each for 1-9 copies, $8.50 for 10 or more.]

Tales of the Heart: Affective Approaches to Global Education by Tom Hampson and Loretta Whalen contains reflective ideas, global education activities, worship materials, and session plans for learning that involves both mind and heart.

[© 1991 by Friendship Press. 244 pages, $19.95. Available from Brethren Press, Elgin, IL 60120 (1-800-441-3712).]

Building a New Community: God's Children Overcoming Racism is a 13-session children's curriculum which includes biblical and contemporary stories, activities, music, worship, with both student and teacher resource.

[© 1992 by Cokesbury. Call Curric-U-Phone, 300-251-8591 from 8:00—4:00, CST, Monday through Friday.]

We All Come from Somewhere
Joshua 24:1-28

*Multiculturalism means we all come from different places.
Like the tribes at Shechem, we each bring a unique
cultural identity and heritage, but we have a common
commitment to God. And because we come from so
many cultures, we express our faith in many colorful
ways that enrich our devotion to God.*

Personal Preparation

1. Read Joshua 24:1-28. Where do you come from? What is
   unique about your heritage?
2. What ethnic or cultural practices do you observe in your
   family?
3. Have you ever moved into another culture to marry, get a
   job, or follow your family? How did you feel in a new and
   different place?
4. What country or culture does your church denomination
   come from? Do you practice any customs of that culture
   in church?

Understanding

Americans struggle in every generation to understand what it
means to be a nation of immigrants. At times we have described
ourselves as a huge melting pot that blends ethnic groups harmoni-
ously into a new mixture. At other times we have celebrated our

individual ethnic extraction, searching for roots and trying to distinguish ourselves from one another. With the recent awareness of the European invasion of Indian cultures in North America, we all have a need to understand what happened when the "old" world met the "new." But each age—the age of the American Revolution, the age of industrialization, the age of slavery, the age of immigration, the age of religious freedom—has found its own meaning for its immigrant status.

Christians in America, as much as anyone, have tried to define what it means to be a nation of immigrants. Turning to the Bible, we have seen a parallel to our own migration in the stories of the Israelites. Early settlers in America and later leaders found in the conquest of Canaan the rationale for the acquisition of the lands of American Indians and for policies such as "manifest destiny." Surely John Winthrop, first governor of colonial Massachusetts, found his rationale in the Bible for starting over in America. In a sermon based on Matthew's Gospel, Winthrop compared the colony that he was about to found to the new Jerusalem. The people who would settle there with him were the chosen people with a divine mission. In a sermon preached aboard the ship Arbella, Winthrop said:

> For we must consider that we shall be a city upon a hill. The eyes of all people are upon us, so that if we shall deal falsely with our God in this work we have undertaken and so cause Him to withdraw His present help from us, we shall be made a story and a byword through the world.

As we study what the Bible says about cultures living together, we must remember that people have used and misused the Bible to justify their ambitions rather than allow the Bible to speak God's word.

The truth is that the Bible neither favors a single culture above others nor promotes a melting pot that is blind to cultural and racial distinctions. In fact, Joshua, who is often cited to justify our feelings of cultural superiority, actually says something very different. He tells us how to live together as many cultures for the glory of God.

When we read this story of the covenant at Shechem, we often think that God is choosing a single group of people called the Israelites over other groups living in Canaan. It is clear, however, that the tribes represented in the covenant were not of one ethnic group. They were many tribes and cultures living in Canaan at the time of the conquest. Apparently God did not choose the people according to their race or culture.

When we suppose that God chooses us because we belong to a certain race or culture, we suppose that we are better than the ordinary person, better than the average human being. That is idolatrous. Like the psalm says, we may be "a little lower than the angels" (Psa. 8:5 KJV), but we are sometimes guilty of elevating ourselves to a little more than God!

So the chosen people all had roots somewhere else. And when they signed on to the covenant at Shechem, they did not try to blend their cultural differences together in a great social melting pot. We have seen what happens when cultures and races are forced to blend. They are not usually successful in forming a new culture with equal parts of your culture and my culture. More often, the new culture takes on the traits of the strongest group. As any cook can tell us, the main ingredient of a recipe stands out. Only when we're part of the main cultural ingredient of society, do we usually like the idea of the melting pot. For instance, the people in a racially homogeneous town may be open-minded about school integration until the children of migrant workers become the largest group of children in the school.

In America we think we are blind to the color of our neighbors. However, denial that we are different is a symptom that something is wrong. It is a mistake to say we are color-blind, that color doesn't matter. To say that we are color-blind is more like saying we are blind to the rich cultures of other people. Too often we can say we love all races and cultures only as long as they have adopted our way of doing things.

Worship, where we assume everyone is welcome and no prejudices exist, is sometimes "the most segregated hour of the week" in America. Church still takes place in ethnic "tribes." From the safety of our congregations where everyone is alike, we can boldly say "there is no longer Jew or Greek, there is no longer slave or free, there is no longer male and female . . . " (Gal. 3:28). Moreover, this verse seems to relieve us from having to try to accept people who are different from us since culture is not important to God.

While culture is not *the* most important characteristic of the new community at Shechem, it is still *an* important characteristic. Notice how Joshua calls each tribe in the covenant by name. But also notice that he does not mention a person's culture as a qualification for signing the agreement. Commitment is the qualification for signing the covenant. These people share a common commitment to God. And because they come from so many cultures, they have many colorful ways to express their faith, each one enriching the devotion to God. This text is important for multicultural faith, because it values our differences while expecting us to live together.

A tribe in Joshua's time was a system of social organization by which things got done—trading, education, defense, and worship. The Book of Judges, which follows Joshua's life, is the story of the tribes of Israel forging a new single society out of necessity. The groups finally came together to take care of their common economic, military, and religious needs. But they did not lose their unique characteristics in the federation. In fact, their history is full of tales about tribal heroes who are "local champions and national figures" such as Gideon, a Manassehite, and Samson, a Danite.

In our day, we sometimes mix up the economic, political, and military reasons for "the tribe" with the religious reasons. When we do that, we come up with all sorts of rationale for taking land, discriminating against others, and staying with our own kind, all in the name of God. We confuse our immigrant path, which we took for political or economic reasons, with a religious cause or mission. Then we are tempted to take our own 20th-century tribalism and project it onto the Hebrew Bible, forcing the Bible into our mold instead of molding ourselves to the Scriptures.

Above all, the people of God at Shechem demonstrate how God wants us to live as a people of faith, not culture. Joshua recites the history of God's mighty acts on behalf of the community (Josh. 24:2-13), showing the rich cultural diversity of Israel's past. He tells God's story to make it evident to hearers that they came to this land as immigrants (vv. 2b-3a), immigrants of various cultures. However, they came not for cultural reasons, but for faith. When God uses an enemy and infidel such as Balaam to bless the Israelites, we know that God is not just presenting an ethnic tale, but a tale of faith.

The purpose of recapping the whole history is to show that the immigration to Canaan was not to deliver a chosen race; it is to point out that we came to the land as recipients of grace. Joshua does not allow us to believe we deserve to have the land because God favors us. In fact, he helps us see we have received the land even though we don't deserve it.

We must also admit that this story of diversity has the potential for terrible pain, pain that comes through this text as we examine its understanding of land. "I brought you . . . [to the land of] the Amorites, the Perizzites, the Canaanites, the Hittites, the Girgashites, the Hivites, and the Jebusites; and I handed them over to you" (Josh. 24:5b, 11b). While faith binds all cultures together, we must also reckon with matters of economic and political justice sooner or later.

The land of Canaan was not uninhabited and had to be conquered for the Israelites. If all people in Canaan had been included in the covenant, we could think of this story as a tribute to multiculturalism alone. But the conquest and covenant at Shechem was a religious agreement between the tribes of Israel, not with the other tribes living in Canaan. The melting pot image may explain the federation of the various tribes of Israel, but it does not do justice to the pagan tribes that lived in the promised land and were driven out.

After Joshua's recital of Israel's history of how they got to Canaan, he tells the people what to do. In a twofold command, Joshua says "Now therefore revere the LORD, and serve him" (24:14). *Revere* in the Hebrew Bible means to acknowledge the fragility of human existence before the power of God. The term *serve* is a broad term meaning "worship." The first term refers to human nature, the second to the divine. In other words, be humble and worship God.

If we "put away the gods that [our] ancestors served beyond the River and in Egypt, and serve the LORD," we reject the pagan gods and recognize that there is one God who alone is powerful. When we fear, we admit the frailty of our culture and our humanness. To be unafraid, on the other hand, is to believe that humans are divine. That is idolatry. And to believe that certain cultures are greater than others is also idolatry. We are called to recognize God's sovereignty and the mere humanness of all cultures.

The text does not allow us the luxury of fence-sitting. Joshua chides us: "Choose this day whom you will serve. . . ." However, the speech does not close with a scolding. It ends with Joshua's confession of what he will do: "But as for me and my household, we will serve the LORD" (Josh. 24:15b). Above all else—our customs, skin color, language, and politics—we will serve the Lord first.

Multicultural faith allows us to hear this same powerful confession with infinite variety, with new richness. It allows us to hear

what God is doing in other cultures. And it brings us to the moment
of choice. Whom shall we serve and revere? Will we serve God or
will we continue to worship our own cultures?

Joshua sent everyone away, each person to his or her inheritance.
He also sent them away with a new inheritance and a new ethnicity,
one in which their varied pasts were not drowned out, but were used
to praise the God of their common faith.

Discussion and Action

1. Tell the group where you came from. Where did your
    ancestors live? How did you come to live where you live?
    What is unique about your heritage?
2. Talk about the writer's statement that God does not pro-
    mote a single best culture or the melting pot idea.
3. After Shechem the people of God continued to live as
    tribes. What bound them together? What binds us together,
    if not the melting pot?
4. The tribes were given the land even though they didn't
    deserve it. And God gives us grace even though we don't
    deserve it. What are some ways that we feel we deserve
    God's favor? What are some reasons we feel God likes our
    culture best?
5. Do a quick inventory of the talents and diversity of your
    Covenant group. Write down your common covenant. You
    are now a culture!

Stephen Breck Reid

2

I'm in Covenant with God, But I'm Not the Only One!
Acts 10:1-48

Knowing that change is coming, the church must say farewell to the end of an era and the loss of some traditions and customs. Then people can move on with joy for the new richness others will bring to our common faith.

Personal Preparation

1. Read Acts 10:1-48. What fears do you have about the church's changing ethnic makeup? What do you dread giving up? What could you give up easily? Which customs of other groups would you find meaningful?
2. Think of a time when you worshiped with another ethnic group. Were you uncomfortable? What did you like about the worship?
3. Like Peter, do you hear God's insisting call, or do you refuse?

Understanding

In my travels, I have seen some interesting variations of Christian worship. Once I stopped in Esquipulous, Guatemala, on a Sunday morning to see the local cathedral and the shrine of the Black Jesus, which was supposed to have healing power. At the time, I was traveling with a caravan of trucks hauling humanitarian aid to Central America and was one of two churchgoers in the group. Another woman driver, who spoke Spanish better than I, drove with me, roomed with me, and talked with me on the long trip. When we reached Guatemala she, a non-Christian, reluctantly agreed to stop with me for a few hours at the cathedral and the shrine.

Being in the cathedral on a Sunday morning was an experience like neither of us had ever had. The cavernous nave was dark and smokey. Hundreds of people filled the space, spreading their blankets on the stone floor to pray. They lit long tapers and shed the first drops of wax on the floor to plant their candles. Then they settled in for long arduous prayer.

In the dim light and thick air, we could see penitents crawling the length of the nave to be forgiven at the shrine near the altar. They began near the centuries-old, carved doors at the back, each one unrolling a blanket ahead of him or herself. They crept forward, making their way from one end of the blanket to the other, then spreading it ahead again, praying without ceasing.

A long line of pilgrims formed outside the church just to see the statue of the Black Jesus through a window behind the altar.

From an inconspicuous aisle, we witnessed this whole vision. It seemed like one of those dreams in which you find yourself in the most unlikely place that only makes sense in the dream. I was invited to take communion but declined, feeling as if I was out of place and would be intruding on someone's important rite. When I remembered that my unchurched friend was with me, I looked around to see her reaction. She looked pale, panicky, and ready to bolt. She said, "I've got to get out of here. I'm scared and I can't breathe." I pushed her through a side door into the sunshine and told her I'd meet her after the mass was over.

It was a strange place for me to be. In my church we put more emphasis on how we live than on how we pray, and our rituals are very practical, not very mystical. But I wanted to stay until the end because I was enraptured, not so much by the ritual as by the tremendous faith I witnessed in the cathedral that day. I had a small revelation at the shrine of the Black Jesus that my church and I are not the only ones who are in covenant with God.

I was reminded that Peter found himself in a weird place too. He had a vision in which meat, forbidden by dietary laws, floated down to him in a billowing sheet. The voice in the vision tells him to break the law and eat the meat. Even though Peter protests, the voice insists that he eat. Sometime after the dream, a Gentile named Cornelius comes to him to learn of Christ and faith. Despite criticism from Jewish authorities who don't want Peter to associate with Gentiles, Peter eats with him and talks to him about Jesus. Their meeting was the beginning of the spread of Christianity to the Gentiles, a sort of second pentecost and the spread of the gospel into the world. Peter, far more than I, was able to venture into a new thing.

The risk for Peter was great. Unlike our world, Peter was part of a minority group that was controlled by an occupying army. The Jews were constantly threatened with extinction by force or annihilation by syncretism, that is, blending with the dominant culture. It was very important for them to maintain a pure practice so that competing religions could not move in and win the hearts and souls of the Jews.

Today, we worry about New Age thinking or cults of various kinds stealing our children away from beloved Christian life. But in the end, we are much different than the Jews of Peter's day. The number of Christians is enormous compared to the numbers involved in cults, and, though cults may be frightening, they do not threaten the institution of the church. But in Peter's time, the Jews were rightly afraid of losing their tradition. Still, Peter, operating at God's command, took the risk to reach out to Gentiles.

Moreover, Peter was reaching out to non-Christians, to people with little knowledge of the gospel. To increase diversity in the church, all we have to do is improve our relationship to other Christians. However, judging from the history of the world in the last 2000 years, we have not been very successful at loving fellow-Christians, let alone the enemy!

Peter responds to Cornelius but not without protest. He was an exemplary Jew and didn't want to be persuaded to do anything contrary to the rules of faith. But God insists. Can we hear God's insisting call today? Or are we so certain of our faith that we would reject God's instruction as Peter did? How can we know what is fundamental in our practice and what should be widened to include others of various backgrounds?

Strangely enough, the modern church has had sanctimonious squabbles over food just as Peter did. In my religious upbringing, the church traditionally used unleavened bread for communion. This bread had to be poked with a fork during baking, and, believe it or not, congregations had major theological disagreements over whether to use a three-tined fork or a four-tined fork to pierce the bread. Then there were debates over communion. Our eucharist is held as part of a reenactment of the last supper in John 13. Churches serve a simple agape meal before the eucharist, but they disagree over what foods should be served. Some serve beef broth and bread; others serve cold meat and fruit. Each church believes it serves the most authentic foods, as though they can serve exactly what Jesus and the disciples would have eaten!

Churches with strong ethnic identity can effectively keep others who do not conform out of fellowship. Nondoctrinal issues such as devotion to language, hymns, food, dress, and traditions keep the church from embracing people of different cultures and ethnicity. Yet some of those things are elemental to who they are. Like Peter, churches are hanging on to tradition in the face of crumbling denominationalism. They cannot and should not stop the change. God is telling all of us to forego the small stuff and to reach out to people who are different from us.

To prepare for the change, we must sort out habitual, customary ethnic practices from those that are central to our faith. While we might keep a particular method of baptism, for instance, we could let go of some of our old favorite hymns to make room for new songs. We do not have to sacrifice the centrality of Jesus Christ to achieve inclusiveness in our worship.

This is not a new thing for the church. The church has had to adjust to God's calling before. Remember that the white church supported slavery for many years. But many denominations changed their position on slavery during the Civil War. They reexamined the rationale for slavery and found it wanting. Now, no church supports involuntary servanthood. Some German immigrant churches had to rethink their loyalty to worshiping in the German language when they moved to the United States. Some that speak Spanish exclusively may have to think of changing in the future. And those that use English will have to provide material in other languages for new members.

The characteristics that make up our identity as a church must be rooted in the gospel and God's calling upon our lives. Particular ethnic practices that enrich our identity become idolatrous when they become the essence of who we are. In my church, too much emphasis on Pennsylvania Dutch language, German hymns, German attention to punctuality, frugality, and cleanliness, and German food at potlucks speaks of an identity that is cultural, not Christian. We have a much richer identity in a New Testament faith that is lived out in response to God's invitation to be part of the kingdom.

I once helped to plan an ecumenical worship service with a committee that was made up largely of people from the Church of Canada. They traditionally held candlelight services for special worship and were well into the plan for a luminated service when someone turned to me and asked if, instead of candlelighting, I could help the group wash feet as we did in my church. Many more people came to the worship than we expected. They wanted to see how feetwashing was done and to participate in it themselves. One hundred fifty people showed up, including a woman in a wheelchair who got her stockings washed as well! People were visibly moved by the practice of humble service and the symbolic and real cleansing embodied in feetwashing.

I was touched by the Canadians' openness to a new thing and the ability of the crowd to find new meaning in the biblical story. Even I dispensed with some of the tradition that has grown up around the feetwashing, such as separating the sexes, wearing prayer coverings, and using unleavened bread, so everyone could be involved in our makeshift setup. It was the raw story we were after in the end anyway.

One of the most important lessons from the Acts scripture is that we cannot capture God. We cannot understand once and for all, not even through the most excellent biblical scholarship. The Jews of Peter's time were excellent scholars. They followed the scriptures to the nth degree. But God did a new thing for them. As Bible scholar William Willimon has said, they were forced to stop asking "Who is God?" and ask "Where is God going now?" If we become too entrenched in our ethnic identity, we will loose track of the God who leads us.

As Christians of any variety, we are after the raw story of God's redemptive love and our call to live in the kingdom. Our different cultures and traditions have added color to the story, but they are not more important than the story itself. The church that can see the difference will understand Peter's defense in front of his peers: "If then God gave them the same gift that he gave us when we believed in the Lord Jesus Christ, who was I that I could hinder God?" (Acts 11:17).

Discussion and Action

1. Talk about your fear of the church's changing ethnic makeup? What does it mean for your church? What could your church give up? What will it gain? Name some of the religious customs that you like in other cultures.

2. When did you first experience another culture? Did you see the value in it then? How were you enriched by the experience?
3. Tell about a time you were in the minority and had to defend your own cultural practices.
4. What do you think is the most important lesson in Acts 10:1-48? Does your congregation practice that teaching?
5. Where is God leading us now? Recall how God led Peter to a new place. Covenant with one other person during this course to take part in another culture. Attend a worship service in another church. Go to an ethnic fair. Invite a family from another country into your home. Teach some songs in another language to your Covenant group. As a whole group, pledge to do one activity together that moves you into a new place.

Julie Garber

3

The Painful Reality of Prejudice
Matthew 15:21-28

Prejudice is the act of judging people based on the group they belong to instead of who they really are. The Canaanite woman who dares to speak to Jesus helps us to get beyond our stereotypes and see the real person.

Personal Preparation

1. Recall your first interracial experience. Was the experience a positive or negative one?
2. Reflect on these definitions. **Prejudice** is judging people based on the group they belong to instead of who they really are. Prejudice usually comes from a stereotype—a false belief that all individuals in a group are the same. **Discrimination** is acting on prejudice. It can take the form of avoiding people, excluding them, or using verbal or physical abuse against them. **Racism** is prejudice and discrimination combined with the power to make decisions that affect people's lives.
3. Think about how you would define *prejudice*. Where have you seen prejudice in your own life?
4. Read Matthew 15:21-28. Do you see any prejudice, discrimination, or racism in the story?

Understanding

I first went to church camp in the early 1960s when I was eight years old. I was one of only five or six African-American children at the denominationally sponsored camp. It was at that camp in the mountains of Southern California that I had what I have come to understand as my first experience of overt racial prejudice.

On the first day of camp, as all of us were lining up to go into the dining room for our first meal, I found myself standing next to a little European-American boy who was my age. As our eyes met, he looked at me and said, "You Negro." I knew from his tone of voice that he was not merely being descriptive. Somehow, he had already gotten the message that to be black was something undesirable and that he could name me and therefore claim a sense of superiority.

As annoying and disturbing as that incident was, it neither threatened my life nor prevented me from returning to church camp and conference and thus to the realization of the redemptive community that can be found in camp and conference.

But the reality of racial prejudice is that for too many people, through evil intention and benign neglect, the effects of prejudice can be deadly.

- In Detroit several years ago, a Chinese-American was beaten to death by two white unemployed auto workers who thought the man was Japanese and therefore responsible for their being out of work.

- In another incident, African-American conventiongoers were stopped by a hotel security guard as they attempted to enter the elevators to go to their rooms. Before they were allowed onto the elevators, they had to show the guard their room keys. European-American conventiongoers were allowed to get on the elevators undisturbed.

In reality, racial prejudice is powerful and affects absolutely all of us. Not even the church of Jesus Christ is immune to its influence. The encounter of Jesus, the disciples, and the Canaanite woman reveals the pervasiveness of our prejudices about race and ethnicity.

A Canaanite woman (a Gentile and an outsider) comes to Jesus for help to heal her daughter who is possessed by a demon. Jesus has a reputation for healing even the most despised people. But at this point the story takes an unexpected and startling twist. When the woman first addresses Jesus, he ignores her and the disciples beg Jesus to send her away. Apparently speaking as if the woman were not present, Jesus says that he was sent only for the lost sheep of Israel, implying that since she is not of his tribe he has no obligation to help her. The woman, in an act of both desperation and subservience, kneels before Jesus and begs for help. It is here that Jesus startles us with what seems like an insulting rebuke. He says, "It is not fair to take the children's food and throw it to the dogs," as if she were a mere animal (Matt. 15:26).

At this point, the woman presses the case with Jesus and becomes the symbol and mentor for every victim of prejudice when she refuses to be limited by the subtle, dehumanizing retort. She is no longer pleading. Now she is arguing a point about the value of a human being: "Yes, Lord, yet even the dogs eat the crumbs that fall from their masters' table" (Matt. 15:27).

Her persistence leads to grace as Jesus declares her a woman of such faith that her wish is granted. With no more than a word from Jesus, her daughter is immediately healed.

The story may lead us to ask if Jesus has been guilty of prejudice, or is he playing some kind of game in which he tests the resolve of the one looking to him for healing? Or better yet, is Jesus offering himself as an example of the way in which prejudice can be overcome?

Matthew's Gospel was written to Christians who no longer understood themselves to be part of the Jewish community. They were urgently forming new traditions and structures to distinguish themselves from their Jewish ancestors, and, at the same time, they were opening themselves and the faith to Gentile converts. Those previously outside the religious culture and despised were to be brought in. So, Matthew's point seems to be that if the Messiah could expand his understanding of who was worthy of his ministry, the community of faith could do no less.

Despite the example of the Gospel, we still have this lesson to learn. Theologian Susan Thistlethwaite was correct when she said in a speech that we are all recovering racists. We are all affected by prejudice, either as victims who must struggle every day to define and love ourselves, or as perpetrators who must struggle every day with an ingrained and misguided notion of racial superiority.

We encounter the painful reality of prejudice too often. We see it in the overrepresentation of African-American and Hispanic men in prison; we see it in the hopelessness of young men and women who have adopted a defeatist attitude that values little and sees no hope in the future. We see it in the code words of "no quotas" and "political correctness" whenever people of different race or ethnicity from our own gain upward mobility. In a nation with a growing non-European population, the realities of racism will grow and become increasingly painful unless all of us, including the church, come to value the gifts each culture brings to church and society.

The Canaanite woman shows us that victims of prejudice do not have to hold onto the effects of bigotry. For the woman, there is a kind of shameless boldness in her approach to Jesus. She does not yield to the prejudice because she understands herself to be a woman worthy of Jesus' attention. The pain of prejudice need not be a permanent condition.

We often hear quoted the "I have a dream" portion of the speech given by Martin Luther King, Jr., at the historic March on Washington in August, 1963. We are proud as we quote the section of the speech in which Dr. King talks about his dream for what the United States could be. But just before he described the dream, he described the reality:

> . . . When the architects of our republic wrote the magnificent words of the Constitution and the Declaration of Independence, they were signing a promissory note to which every American was to fall heir. It is obvious today that America has defaulted on this promissory note insofar as her citizens of color are concerned. Instead of honoring this sacred obligation, America has given the Negro people a bad check, a check which has come marked "insufficient funds." We refuse to believe the bank of justice is bankrupt. So we have come to cash this check—a check that will give us upon demand the riches of freedom and the security of justice.

Only after the reality of prejudice is acknowledged and honestly described can we speak of dreams, and only as we work to make our dreams come true, can we overcome the bitter realities that leave us mired in the sinfulness of prejudice.

Discussion and Action

1. Review Matthew 15:21-28 together. What prejudices or racism do you see in this story? How does Jesus deal with the prejudice?
2. Examine your own congregation and your denomination. Where do you see prejudice?
3. Identify your racial prejudices. What would it be like for you to be friends with someone from a group you think is inferior?
4. Describe a time when you displayed your prejudices.
5. Have you been a victim of racial prejudice? Share as much as you choose about a personal encounter with racial prejudice.
6. How do you think prejudice is understood in countries other than the United States?

LaTaunya M. Bynum

4

The Struggle with Racism
Ezra 9—10; Acts 15:1-35

Racism is the use of power to isolate, separate, and exploit others. As Paul and Barnabas discovered, the church is guilty of separating Christians along racial and ethnic lines, despite good intentions. Like the early church, we must examine our attitudes on race and open the church doors to all.

Personal Preparation

1. As you read the biblical texts, note the things that seem strange or unacceptable to you, and summarize your understanding of both passages.
2. Recall your most significant experiences involving people of another racial or ethnic identity. Try to understand how the experiences came about and how they have influenced your actions toward people different from you.
3. List your own race-related issues, describing the pain and struggle involved.
4. Identify the power issues in the Understanding section below that most concern your congregation as a covenant community.

Understanding

I grew up in an all white church singing: "Jesus loves the little children, All the children of the world. Red and yellow, black and white, They are precious in his sight. Jesus loves the little children of the world." Of course, all the children I was singing with were the white ones. Later in my childhood, one "brown" (we didn't yet have that category) and one yellow person joined that church. It was years before a black person was welcomed and still there are no red people. But now the world is changing.

One predominantly white, middle-class denomination in the US is predicting that its power struggles will shift from doctrinal fights to ethnic demands for greater representation and sharing of power (Theodore E. Mall, "Trends 2000," Southern Baptist Convention, 1990, p. 6.). The shift reflects changes in the general population, in which "the percentage of Anglos in the USA will decrease while the Asian, Hispanic, and Black population will increase dramatically" (Mall, p. 2).

European-American churches will find themselves in a situation not unlike that of Ezra and the Israelites who returned to their promised land after years of captivity in Babylon to find that many non-Jews and people of other cultures were inhabiting their lands. To preserve the purity of their community, the Israelites discriminated against the other cultures and religions, forcing out the foreign wives and children. The church historically has discriminated on the basis of race. How the church feels about multiculturalism today and how it responds to the challenge to accept other races and cultures may decide its future.

The church has always struggled with issues of inclusion and exclusion. Racism, which has been on the agenda of the North American church since the days of slavery through the Civil Rights Movement, continues to be at the top of the list of these issues. In the debate, European-Americans have sometimes appropriated the Bible and Jesus as their own; yet this book is the covenant of diverse peoples, whose Savior, Jesus, was clearly not a middle-class North American. The reality is that, despite good intentions, projects, and programs, many Christians are still racists and more prone to exclusion rather than inclusion, using power and authority to exclude certain people. Churches and people of faith need now more than ever to address both personal and corporate racism in a forthright way.

Consider this definition:

> Racism is the intentional or unintentional use of power
> to isolate, separate and exploit others. This use of power
> is based on a belief in superior racial origin, identity, or

supposed racial characteristics. Racism confers certain privileges on and defends the dominant group, which in turn sustains and perpetuates racism. Both consciously and unconsciously, racism is enforced and maintained by the legal, cultural, religious, educational, economic, political and military institutions of societies. Racism is more than just a personal attitude, it is the institutionalized form of that attitude. (Policy Statement on Racial Justice of the National Council of Churches of Christ, U.S.A.)

Racism, as described above, is perhaps best reflected biblically in the attitudes and actions of the Pharaoh and the Egyptians toward the Hebrews during the years of slavery prior to the Exodus. We are familiar with that story. Other scriptures describe similar institutionalized attitudes, usually between cultures and religions rather than races. Ezra and Acts, particularly, deal with how the Jewish prophets and authorities treated non-Jews. Neither book contains religious laws or rules for the treatment of outsiders; rather, each comes at discrimination from an emotional, visceral response. As in the preceding definition of racism, the treatment of others is based not on rational criteria but on a mere belief that one group is superior or that encroaching foreigners will rob them of their identity.

Judaism after the Exile found itself in a multicultural situation that threatened its very existence. At least that is how the writer of Ezra saw it. When the Persian king, Cyrus, released the Jewish exiles, they went home to the promised land. In an effort to reestablish the Jews as the people of God, religious leaders forbad mixed marriages between Jews and other inhabitants of the land. For the leaders, it was a purity issue—the land was unclean and so were the people who had moved in. That is, they did not keep the law. The "holy seed," or purity of blood line of the faithful people of the covenant, was not to be mixed with that of people who had committed the abomination of worshiping idols. The priest Ezra prayed, asking forgiveness for Israel's sin of disobedience. The people responded by sending away their foreign wives and their children. They anguished over the difficult choice between justice for rejected wives and children and obedience to God.

Centuries later, Jesus' followers were still concerned about their religious survival. Jesus, however, had undermined the traditional assumptions of leaders, dismissing physical purity laws (see Mark 7:1-23) while retaining the importance of purity of heart.

Acts 15 portrays early church leaders as they too wrestled with the problem of who could be included in the faith. Paul and Barnabas had invited Gentiles into the covenant community, believing that the good news was for the whole world and that Gentiles had received the Holy Spirit in the same way as did Jews (compare Acts 2 with Acts 10). But eventually the question arose: Do Gentiles have to keep the purity laws of the Torah to be obedient? The Jerusalem church leaders, who had the only real authority, decided that Gentiles did not have to keep the laws, but they asked the Gentiles to keep away from some pollutants: food sacrificed to idols, fornication, meat strangled, and blood. Gentile abstinence was a compromise that would make them acceptable to the Jewish believers.

Lest we think that the church today is free of such requirements, we can point to ways that the church protects its identity much as the Hebrews of Ezra's time did. Consider baptism. What would we do if Christian leaders today began to argue for including people in the church without requiring the ritual of baptism? Already many churches accept new members on the basis of their baptism in another denomination, even if the baptism was performed by another method. How far are we from dispensing with baptism in favor of a confession of faith?

These two stories challenge us to imagine ourselves as the wives and children of Jews in Ezra's time or Gentiles who were kept out by the policies and laws of the community trying to preserve itself. They also challenge us to review our own churches and policies that may be keeping people out in subtle or overt ways because of race or culture. We can feel the pain of excluded people and take up their cause. With them we share the pain of racism and the struggle to overcome racism's devastating effects. It is a struggle that affirms first of all that every human is made in God's image and held in God's infinite love. Having proclaimed that, we can all make changes to ensure full participation of any who know the grace of God.

Discussion and Action

1. As a group, identify with the wives and children who were turned away by their husbands and fathers in the Ezra

passage. List the words that first come to mind. Describe their pain as you imagine it.

2. Using the Acts passage, identify with new Gentile Christians who had received the good news and believed they were fully part of the faith, only to find that some church leaders believed that Gentiles could not be Christians. How would you feel? List your responses.

3. Identify the painful feelings from both lists, and discuss how they relate to the pain inflicted by racism. How are they like and unlike racism in our society, churches, and personal experiences?

4. Examine the definition of racism in this session. Choose the phrase that seems most important to you and tell the group why you think so.

5. How have prejudices identified in the previous session been institutionalized in your church? How has the racial makeup of your community and your church changed in recent years? Does anyone in your church have the power or influence to keep others out?

6. Given the anticipated changes in population cited in Understanding, what fears do you have? What is a creative response?

7. What are your church's attitudes about baptism? Is baptism an outward symbol of inward change? Is it a sacrament that cannot be compromised? How closely does it compare to ritual circumcision as a way to preserve the church?

8. What could your group do to demonstrate a commitment to the church as a racism-free community? How would the dynamics of your Covenant group be changed if the racial makeup were different?

Phillip E. Hoyle

5

Decision: Preserving or Risking?
Matthew 15:21-28

The story of the Syrophoenician woman illustrates the terrible pain of prejudice and rejection. As this session notes, the story also shows Jesus as a person who will take great risks to include an outsider.

Personal Preparation

1. Reread the story of the Syrophoenician woman (Matt. 15:21-28) and consider why Jesus responded as he did.
2. What in your faith is most precious to you? What would you consider only peripheral?
3. Who are the outsiders in your community who are like the Syrophoenician woman?
4. Read the stories of Peter at Joppa (Acts 10—11:18) and Paul on the way to Damascus (Acts 9:1-22).

Understanding

The world in which we live constantly brings people of different cultures and races together. Some sociologists are saying that within 30 years white people of European descent will be a minority in the United States. Few urban communities are exempt from the immigration of people from Hispanic and Asian cultures. African-Americans already live in most communities in this country. Even rural communities will hardly be able to resist these trends.

People in the world of Jesus' day were also coming together from many different races and cultures. The conquest of Alexander the Great created a new world environment that was enhanced by the Roman empire. Christianity itself was born as a new community dedicated to God, which included peoples of many heritages. The struggle to come to this new vision is at the heart of the New Testament.

In session 3, LaTaunya Bynum looked at the story of the Syrophoenician woman as an example of the tremendous pain of discrimination. In this session, we will look more specifically at Jesus' role in the story to see how an insider, someone who enjoys acceptance already, responds to the outsider. The Syrophoenician woman (Matt. 15:21-28) was from a culture whose people did not worship the God of Abraham. In Hebrew eyes these people were heathen. When she asked Jesus to heal her daughter, he gave the conventional answer, an answer that illustrates how human it is to participate in the cultural and racial biases of our time. Jesus said, "It is not fair to take the children's [Israel's] food and throw it to the dogs."

Her response to him brought Jesus up short: "Yet even the dogs eat the crumbs that fall from their masters' table," she said. Seeing the woman's faith, Jesus granted her request. The common view that Syrophoenicians were infidels (literally, unfaithful) no longer fits. Like the Samaritan who stopped to care for someone who had been attacked on the highway, and like the Roman centurion who asked only that Jesus give the command to heal his daughter, this Syrophoenician woman showed faith uncommon even in Israel. In all three instances Jesus witnessed the unusual faith of people who were not among the insiders.

When those who are of other races and traditions challenge those of us who are insiders, we are driven to reconsider the true meaning of our faith. Such challenges bring us to deeper concerns about the inclusive availability of God's healing salvation.

However, such inclusiveness often comes with great risk, often with great pain, and often with embarrassment. When Jesus was approached by the Syrophoenician woman, his first response was to emphasize his primary mission to the people of Israel. Her challenge and Jesus' ultimate response make it clear that his more fundamental mission is to all people who are willing to be faithful.

When we are challenged by newcomers of other races and cultures, we too must decide what is to be preserved and what may be given up for the sake of a deeper vision of faith. What is essential and what is peripheral? Often the decision involves an identity crisis. Remember Peter at Joppa wrestling with the question of whether he could eat with those who ate "unclean food." Or consider Paul's experience on the road to Damascus when he realized that Jesus' message was for all people, not just the Jews. After their experiences, they had to question which Mosaic traditions were to be continued and which had to be sacrificed. The inclusion of people of other cultures and races brings risk, even to the point of an identity crisis. It was in such encounters that the New Testament revelation was born. The question of what to preserve and what to risk for the sake of a deeper faith is on each page of the New Testament.

The perspective of the New Testament is that everyone who receives God's forgiveness is joined together in a community of the faithful to live a joyful life of care for one's neighbors, risking what is necessary to overcome enmity and injustice while being guided by Christ's Spirit through prayer, Bible study, experience, and understanding. Customs, rituals, habits, traditions, and liturgies develop in the faith community, but they are all subject to challenge by encounters with new people. The only real question is whether insiders and outsiders are willing to accept God's forgiveness and live within the perspective of the New Testament. All else is dressing.

Several years ago the pastor of a small congregation developed a "school of Christian living," a six-week course about the church. The school was well-attended, with four or five new families coming to the church. Members of the congregation were elated to have them. They had tried for years to expand their numbers but had never been able to do so.

Two of the families became particularly faithful in attendance and active in church events. When the next church election occurred, a member from each of these two families was elected to the church board. Because the church was small, membership on the church board seldom changed. The election of two newcomers meant two of the old-timers were not reelected. Within several months after the election, members of the families of those who had been replaced dropped out of the church. The result was the membership of the congregation returned to about the same number as it was before the school of Christian living.

People in this congregation thought they wanted new members, but they were not willing to let newcomers have a place in the decision-making of the church. The presence of new families brought on an identity crisis for other families and they left. In the New Testament we are called to be willing to worship, commune, and serve one another. We are to listen to what Christ is saying to us as we encounter the new relationships God is bringing about among us.

Churches can be welcoming without losing their identity or forcing others to conform to their traditions. A young friend of mine married a woman from another Christian tradition, and they struggled with where they should attend church. A very large and active independent church was located within a block of their home. The young woman loved attending Bible studies there. The church of his denomination was small and relatively unknown in that community. However, they decided to go there, and that congregation did everything they could to make the young woman feel loved and accepted by Jesus Christ and themselves. The church made a place for them and they became very active members.

Many people in my denomination, the Church of the Brethren, feel the church has been pure and unadulterated since its beginning in 1708 in Schwarzenau, Germany. In reality the church has been influenced constantly by the traditions around it. Born of Pietism and Anabaptism, early Brethren were also influenced by the Calvinists and the Lutherans. The Quakers invited the Brethren to this country and were influential in the plain style of life that developed among Brethren. Missions, church schools, and many practices have been adopted from other traditions. I am sure the same could be said for most denominations.

Key to the New Testament church is the willingness to worship together, pray together, study the Scriptures together, commune together, and in doing so, to seek the living presence and mind of Jesus Christ. It was the Syrophoenician woman's faith that so struck Jesus, a kind of faith he seldom encountered in Israel. Such faith is not pushy or demanding but is, at the same time, assertive and confident in and through its trust in Jesus. We will always be jarred by the encounter with new traditions, but Jesus shows us how to meet such encounters and how to preserve what is necessary and risk what is peripheral to bring the outsider in.

Discussion and Action

1. When have you given up a cherished belief and then discovered a deeper faith? Share these experiences with one another.

2. Which of your congregation's current practices are peripheral? Which do you see as essential?

3. Christians have sought to live according to the New Testament. What are the essential elements of New Testament faith? Develop a group list. Compare your list to that given in the last paragraph of the lesson. Discuss the points where the two lists differ.

4. Who in your community is an outsider like the Syrophoenician woman?

5. In what ways are you personally now being called to risk? What are you learning about faith?

6. How is your church or denomination being called to risk? What are you learning?

7. Look at the small, imperceptible changes in your church over the decades. How is the church different? How is it the same? What threads carry through the history of your church?

Donald E. Miller

6

"Those Far Off...
Now Brought Near"
Ephesians 2:11-22

Everyone is an insider in the eyes of God. That is the good news. The crucial task for Christians today is to break down walls in the church, in families, in ourselves that keep out the people God wants us to bring in.

Personal Preparation

1. Think of one custom, style of dress, food, or lifestyle from another culture in or out of our country. How would such a custom affect the life of your fellowship, your congregation, or your church group if a person of that culture joined?
2. Name a custom that aggravates you. Be honest. How will you prayerfully come to accept that custom?
3. Read Ephesians 2:11-22. The symbol of "a dividing wall" was based on an actual wall that separated two ethnic groups, Jew and Greek, at the old temple in Jerusalem. A sign warned Gentiles on pain of death to stay on their side. What walls have been erected against you in your life? How did they make you feel?
4. Recall the familiar song "This Little Light of Mine," a spiritual from the slave experience in the United States, yet we all sing it. In what ways do you resist the melding of cultures? When do you find it challenging and exciting?

Understanding

The twelve partners of the European Community hope to abolish frontiers and begin free commerce. One of their biggest obstacles has turned out to be time, not time zones, but attitudes toward time. When it comes to doing business together their cultural differences over schedules stand in the way.

Scandinavians, Swiss, and Germans are at work by 8 a.m. British executives don't generally make calls before 10:30 a.m. The Italian government works six days a week, but northern Europeans don't like anything to infringe on their two-day weekends. Muslims, a growing European force, consider Friday their sabbath. Spaniards and Greeks take a siesta between 2 and 5 p.m. Some Italians leave for lunch at 2:00 and do not come back until the next day. Northern Europeans are punctual. Mediterranean countries tend to be less precise about time. No one is right or wrong. They just have different ways of doing things.

These are all western cultures with cultural affinities. Despite a strong desire to unify economically, they find it difficult to become one people.

But even within a single country, cultural barriers divide people. In California something as simple as an address can become a stumbling block to an ethnic group. Imagine a medical building with a street address of 9413 Elm Street. A Chinese person who speaks the Mandarin or Cantonese dialect might hesitate to enter such a building, because the numerals in those languages have other meanings. The numbers 9, 4, 1, and 3 also mean "Nine die, one lives." The number 664 becomes "continuous death," while 424 becomes "die and die again." The number 148, on the other hand, means "a lifetime of prosperity." In the city of Los Angeles there is a thriving trade in changing addresses and phone numbers for immigrants who desire lucky numbers.

Think of some of the different customs you have encountered in your own experience. Try to imagine a church in which all these various customs are observed. The inability of similar countries, or even people within a single country, to come together makes us wonder whether anyone can bring such disparate groups together.

Paul's message in Ephesians is that indeed there is one who can hold us together even when we resist. "So then you are no longer strangers and aliens, but you are citizens . . . of the household of God . . . with Christ Jesus himself as the cornerstone" (2:19, 20).

Or as it is put in 1 Peter 2:10: "Once you were not a people, but now
you are God's people. . . . "

These are Paul's comforting words to Gentiles who were rejected
by the Jews. When they tried to enter the temple, this sign in Greek,
the language of the Gentiles, effectively kept them out and unwelcome:

> No foreigner is to go beyond the balustrade and the plaza
> of the temple zone. Whoever is caught doing so will
> have himself to blame for his death which will follow.

It is easy for us to forget that the barrier between Jew and Gentile
was as much an ethnic barrier as a religious one. It came down to
differences between the clean and the unclean. Distinctions were
made between what meat could be eaten, how it could be slaugh-
tered, and how it could be prepared. We are like the Jews, prisoners
of our upbringing, and sometimes the sight of alien food brings on
the gag reflex. It is terribly difficult not to judge another's way as
inferior.

Yet Scripture from the beginning has praised the contribution of
the outsider. Melchizedek, for instance, was the priest of a pagan
god, yet his communion with Abraham made him the model for the
perfect priest, Jesus Christ (Gen. 14:18-20 and Heb. 7:1-17). The
first prayer recorded in Scripture belongs not to an important
patriarch, but to a nameless slave who trusts God to give him a sign
in seeking a wife for his master's son (Gen. 24:12-14). Tamar (Gen.
38) and Rahab (Matt. 1:5) and Ruth (Ruth 4:13, 18-22), all foreigners, become part of the royal Davidic line and, by extension,
ancestors of Jesus. Ruth, especially, is lifted up as a source of
blessing and an example to the faithful everywhere—yet she is one
of the hated Moabites, and her marriage with Boaz is precisely the
sort of interracial marriage of which Ezra disapproved (Ezra 10:1-5).

Jesus' ministry clearly hammers away at the walls that divide
God's people. He speaks freely with the Samaritan woman at the well
(John 4). She is able to banter with Jesus where theologian Nicode-
mas falters. Jesus praises the centurion, an officer in the hated
occupying army, for displaying faith unsurpassed by anyone in Israel
(Matt. 8:5-10). And when Greeks are brought to him during passion
week, he proclaims, "For this I came into the world" (John 18:37).

The road to diversity is not easy for us, but with God's grace all
things are possible. The Book of Acts is testament to that. Its
twenty-eight chapters are full of examples of feuding and fussing

over what are essentially ethnic and cultural issues. Paul's Letter to the Ephesians speaks of how "the dividing wall" has been broken down (2:14). This dividing wall has both symbolic and literal meaning. There was the dividing wall that kept Gentile and Jew apart in the temple worship. People of the nations, weary of the confusing polytheism of their day, could become "Godfearers," professing a belief in the one God, but they could draw only so close to the great drama enacted within the temple proper. The wall threatened them with death if they passed beyond. The blood of Christ figuratively tore down that wall and made possible a whole new set of problems and opportunities as Christians came to terms with their separate customs.

Consider the Berlin Wall, only recently destroyed, something I did not believe I would live to see. It was a great blessing as people long separated were brought together. Yet, with it came a multitude of problems, as people living under differing economic systems came to grips with the problems of skills, job motivation, unemployment, and fears about savings. Yet these are blessed problems, far preferable to a world divided by fear and suspicion, perpetually on the brink of nuclear war.

Making assumptions, though often innocently, is an easy way to build walls. A woman called me to ask for instructions regarding an upcoming carry-in dinner at church. I had assumed everyone knew how they worked! On another occasion I phoned a Lebanese family to see if they'd be attending our Fourth of July celebration. They figured that since we called the dinner an All-American Dinner they weren't allowed! With my explanation and encouragement they came and had a great time.

We sometimes assume it would be easier to exist separate but equal in God's eyes. I read the newsletter of an African-American church in Detroit whose pastor insisted that African-Americans belong solely in single-race churches. I reject the notion. With the example of our forebears, we should courageously embrace the problems of mixing social background, language, economic differences, and prejudice of all sorts. We should, in fact, seek out and welcome people different from us into our fellowships.

That doesn't mean it won't be tough. But with the wall between races down, we are beset with blessed problems. One time my eight-year-old daughter and I decided to take a German guest to the installation of a pastor at a church near South Central Los Angeles. I warned them both it might take as long as two hours. It took nearly four hours for the largely black congregation to finish the service! Ironically, the length and style of the service was much closer to the earliest style of worship in my denomination than the way we do it now.

Perhaps someday we will grow to be the church that God intends, with no national boundaries, with congregations all over the world. Our members will speak different tongues and live different lives, but we will all proclaim the same risen Lord.

Discussion and Action

1. Share some of the different customs you thought of this week, including those that aggravate you.
2. Name some of the walls that keep you out of the "inside." When have you participated in erecting such walls?
3. Name some times in church when you have experienced Jesus Christ bringing insiders and outsiders together.
4. Imagine you are part of a multi-ethnic church that includes fellowships around the world. What changes would you and your denomination be willing to make, including relocating headquarters and meeting places to accommodate this vision?
5. Pray together for the courage to erase long held prejudices or assumptions. Write them on a piece of paper and then have a ceremony to burn them or tear them up. Ask God to transform you even as the Ephesians and the first-century church prayed to be transformed.

Frank Ramirez

7

All Ate and Were Satisfied
Matthew 14:13-21

Diverse groups need opportunities to work, study, eat, and worship together in an atmosphere where people are willing to listen, able to see possibility in the stranger, and instinctively tune their ears to hear what others have to say. The Bible calls this atmosphere "hospitality."

Personal Preparation

1. Think about times when you attended an activity and felt welcome. What made the event particularly hospitable? Think about times when you attended an activity and felt alienated or left out. Why did you not feel welcome?
2. What feelings and thoughts does the word *community* bring to mind? What is your idea of an ideal community to visit? What is your idea of an ideal community to live in?
3. It is often said that to love others one must start with oneself. How does this thought relate to hospitality and sharing? How is the love of God related to loving ourselves and others?
4. Read Matthew 14:13-21. Which parts of this scripture exemplify hospitality? Which parts exemplify community? What makes the meal satisfying?

Understanding

The passage on the feeding of the five thousand combines several important themes in Jesus' teachings: community, hospitality, and the coming together of the family of God. Despite the disciples' reluctance, Jesus assembles the crowd that begs for his healing touch. As their host, he heals them and feeds them until they are satisfied. When they are through, the disciples collect twelve baskets of leftover bread, a possible symbol of the twelve tribes of Israel who ate bread in the wilderness and joined together to form God's people.

By example, Jesus teaches the disciples about drawing the people of God together to satisfy their needs for healing and their hunger to belong to God. Christians have enormous ministries in community development and hospitality; however, as the Lord leads the church into a more and more culturally and ethnically diverse world at home and abroad, we are faced with our culturally ingrained sins of racism and prejudice.

Community is formed out of life together. But as disciples of Christ, we have two lives. The first life is within our church community with our sisters and brothers. The second is our life in the world. Christian writer Harold S. Bender says that "in church there are no classes, no clergy and laity, no artificial distinctions, but a fellowship of equals" and that when true Christian community exists, "then all the resources of every member will be enlisted for the common work of the church and to meet the several needs of all" (*The Anabaptist Vision*). This vision is a challenge to every one of us.

As we serve our Lord in this volatile world, we desperately need all the help we can get. But we often forego chances God gives us to broaden our associations with new and different people, and we stick with people just like us. We think they are "easier" to get to know and work with. We often treat the church as our own "personal" retreat from the world, instead of a place where God's children of every nationality, ethnicity, race, and social class can work together to build up the kingdom on earth. We are like the disciples who were eager to follow Jesus as long as they didn't have to be bothered by the needy people who always congregated around Jesus. How often have we actually tried to serve God with all the resources available to us (the time, talents, and economic resources of our churches and surrounding neighborhoods)? It isn't always easy to discover or use to full purpose the tools the Lord has available, but it is something we must take to heart and learn if we are to serve Jesus.

I live at Reba Place, a church community in Evanston, Illinois. Many of the families and single members of the church live within a six square block area of the city. Some make their living providing services such as child care, social work, and care for the elderly. We live a shared and simple life, giving our lives totally to Jesus. But as a graduate student at Northwestern University's Kellogg Graduate School of Management, I live in a second world and feel the pressures of both church and school. At school, I am tempted by the worldly demands for prestige, popularity, and monetary success. At Reba I feel the demands of the church to be a servant, to live simply, to live for others.

When I first started to get involved, fellow students frequently asked why a "business type" was interested in attending a church full of seminary graduates and social workers. My brothers and sisters at church seemed to question whether it was possible to serve the Lord in an environment where the world's values were applauded and worshiped. I can attest to the fact that it is a constant challenge, and the only way I am able to survive is with the help of the Christian community I live in and the constant support the Lord gives me personally.

Because of the acceptance and support I get from the church, I am able to reach out to fellow students and the community at large by working in organizations such as Business with a Heart. Business with a Heart is my school's charity and volunteer organization, which works with soup kitchens, a homeless shelter, and food-drive programs.

Sometimes it isn't clear why the Lord places us in the specific faith and world communities we are in, especially when they seem so polar opposite, but each situation the Lord directs us to is certain to be important to our development as disciples of our Lord Jesus.

Jesus emphasized sharing and hospitality when the disciples asked what to do with the five thousand. In fact, he directed the disciples to "give them something to eat" and when they could not do this, Jesus said "bring them to me" (Matt. 14:16-18 NIV) and then proceeded to set the foundation for how we are to offer hospitality. In the style of the eucharist, Jesus first gave thanks, then he gave the food to his disciples to serve the masses. That little bit of food went a long way. "They all ate and were satisfied." Even though the people were starved for the nourishment Jesus had to offer, the disciples hesitated to be hospitable. But Jesus used the disciples. He worked through them to administer the task, breaking down their resistance to community with the crowd.

When the disciples say to Jesus, "Send the crowds away," I think about how we respond to overwhelming needs, saying to our Lord, "Send the crowds away." Our hearts have already abandoned the idea of offering hospitality because we feel overburdened and needy ourselves. But I know what it's like to be rebuffed by good people who cannot be hospitable. I can remember feeling not too welcome a few times visiting a new church. I would be greeted by a few of the church members with a smiling nod. Most would ignore me, while one or two would energetically welcome me to the new church. On following visits to the new church, I would be treated with the same reception I received the first time or be ignored totally. During these times I would feel like a stranger in God's house, unknown and invisible to my brothers and sisters.

Now that I have been a Christian for a number of years, I have observed myself giving newcomers the same reception I received so many times, giving them a smile or a brief introduction and maybe an obligatory "so what do you do and where are you from?" Frequently, they would want to engage me further in discussions, to get to know me better, but I would politely excuse myself after a few minutes because I would have things to do that afternoon. During these times I would feel Jesus urging me to spend more time with this "stranger"; but I would just sigh and tell Jesus, "I am too tired to offer myself to this person, besides I have important work to do for you," promptly forgetting that Jesus taught me "to do unto others what you would have them do unto you." By not aligning my "heart" with God's purpose for me, I am not always able to be a brother to other Christians.

There may be political, economic, or military barriers to offering hospitality to the masses, but the greatest barrier is our unwillingness. If we can't open our hearts at least to commune together over a simple meal, then we don't allow our Lord to work through us. Henri Nouwen, in his book *The Three Movements of the Spiritual Life: Reaching Out*, talks about the need to reach out to our fellow human beings and to move from hostility to hospitality. In offering hospitality, Henri Nouwen says that we create space for the strangers so they can enter and be free to "cast off their strangeness" and "sing their own songs, speak their own languages, dance their own dances; free also to leave and follow their own vocations." In essence "hospitality is not a subtle invitation to adopt the life style of the host, but the gift of a chance for the guest to find his own."

Once we have opened our hearts to hospitality we are to give thanks first before starting our work for the Lord, in the same way Jesus gave thanks for what the Lord provided. Central to the idea of hospitality is the feeling of gratitude, both for what others have to offer us and what we have to offer our neighbors. Too often I look to myself and feel inadequate and ill-equipped to do the Lord's work. I have to remind myself constantly that when I am weak the Lord is strong. The Lord, however, is able to use the most insignificant of my talents to glorify him if I thank him for that gift and then offer it to him in service. Like the child who offered the five loaves of bread and the two little fish (John 6:8-10), the Lord finds great joy in the small offerings we make in his name and blesses that action by multiplying it a thousandfold.

A simple meal can begin to break down barriers and allow community to be formed. Like the diversity in the crowd of five thousand, diversity enriches our neighborhoods, but only when we embrace diversity and welcome it will we have true community. Once we have invited our new friends, we need to be patient and allow for time and opportunity to work, study, eat, and worship together. We need to create an atmosphere where there is a willingness to listen, an ability to see possibility in the stranger, and an impulse to tune our ears to hear what the disenfranchised have to say. In this way we allow God to work through us as little children to achieve through us what we are incapable of achieving on our own.

Discussion and Action

1. Share your thoughts from question 1 in Personal Preparation. Talk about a time when you were invited to a meal or an activity and felt unwelcome or left out.
2. Look at Matthew 14:13-21. Where do you find hospitality in this passage? What brings about a sense of community in the story? Why were all satisfied?
3. Tell of a time when you felt like the disciples and wanted to dismiss the needy. Tell of a time when you were able to

offer hospitality and share in someone else's adversity. How did you feel in each case?

4. Consider your faith community and your community in the world. What struggles do you have with each? How does the Lord use you in each community? How do you provide hospitality in each one? How can you bring the two worlds closer together?

5. Often, stereotypes and judgments hold us back from reaching out to others. List the diverse groups of people (e.g., ethnic, racial, cultural, occupational, denominational, economic, etc.) in your neighborhood. Then list your stereotypes and judgments about each group. From which group do you feel the most estranged or alienated? How might you reach out to them?

6. What new understanding have you gained about community and hospitality? How can you put your learning into action? Plan for your Covenant group to share a meal with a true variety of people, or plan a service project at a homeless shelter or hospitality house.

Charles H. Kwon

8

"How They Love Each Other"
John 13:1-17

Diversity in the church requires more than simple inclu-
siveness or inviting others "in" to be part of "us." It
requires mutuality. The feetwashing in John 13 is our
example for giving our gifts and receiving the gifts of
others.

Personal Preparation
1. Read the text from John three times. Find the verses that
   speak of practical love. Look up the definition of love in a
   Bible dictionary. Think of ways you can put love into
   practice in your life.
2. In what ways did Jesus put into practice God's commandment to love?
3. Do you think that feetwashing is a commandment of love?
   How easy is it for you to give to others and receive from
   others? Read John 13:14-15. What do these verses mean
   for us today?

Understanding
The term *love* seems cheap these days, especially when it denotes
only the most base physical love such as we see in the movies and
on prime time television. With the constant bombardment of lusty
entertainment, we forget sometimes that there are other varieties of
love, love that is respectful and selfless and love that is divine. As

the cultures of the world have more frequent contact and grow more and more to depend on each other, they must seek these forms of love. Without love the world will devour itself in hatred, selfishness, and greed.

In the scripture from the Gospel of John, Jesus instructs us in love by example. In the act of washing feet, Jesus shows us what mutual love is. He does not require us to love as God loves for we are merely mortal. And though Jesus was fully divine, Paul said of him that "he did not regard equality with God as something to be exploited, but emptied himself, taking the form of a slave, being born in human likeness" (Phil. 2:6, 7). So, as a slave, he kneeled before Peter and washed his feet.

If the church is to truly follow Christ, it must embody this kind of mutual love, following the commandment to "love one another as I have loved you" (John 15:12). We are good at mutual love with people who are just like we are. But when it comes to relating with people different than we are, our love becomes lopsided. We think we can heal cultural and ethnic divisions in the church if we simply open our church doors and pour out our love on "foreigners." But unless love is mutual and we are able to receive love as well as give it, we will not have followed Jesus' command or succeeded in honoring the stranger in our midst who has something to bring to the church.

Jesus, knowing that one of his own followers would betray him, still wanted love to be mutual between them. When he offered himself freely, he did it both as an example of how we are to give love as well as how we are to receive love, particularly his love. The meaning of the last supper is complete only when both dimensions are included.

It has been more than a year since my husband and I came to Santa Ana, California, to pastor a growing congregation of Spanish-speaking people, mostly Mexicans. We meet in a church that belongs to a small white congregation of the same denomination, made up of mostly elderly people who have remained in the Mexican neighborhood long after most European-Americans have moved to other neighborhoods.

This beloved English-speaking congregation opened their doors to us, not only those to the sanctuary and facilities, but the doors of their hearts as well. Our Mexican congregation calls them "grand people." To us it is a pretty phrase because age in the children of

God demonstrates the "grandness" of maturity, service, patience, and love.

By their generosity, we are able to make ourselves at home in their building. We use the sanctuary for worship, one of the rooms for clothing for the needy, an office for counseling those with emotional or spiritual needs, and classrooms for Bible study and English lessons, classes that help children and adults face the problems of life in this country.

The English-speaking congregation did not invite us into their worship and expect us to adopt their language, their style of worship, and their favorite hymns. They made room for us to be ourselves, to bring our special gifts to the church and to be a part of their praying and worshiping community.

Too often, we think that Jesus commanded us only to be servants. We try running around taking care of everyone else, never letting anyone take care of us. We are like Peter who was opposed to Jesus washing his feet. Peter felt he should be the servant. The Savior of the world should not kneel to wash feet. Peter was slow in understanding what his master was teaching him. Upon completing the feetwashing, Jesus gave the full instruction that included both serving and being served: "You also ought to wash one another's feet" (John 13:14-15).

Healing happens in the mutuality of feetwashing. We serve others and we allow others to touch us and change us, cleanse us and make us whole. The slave image is appropriate because slaves need healing for their divided lives. They give all to nurse and nurture their masters and at the same time are extremely needy, being without rights, property, and freedom.

Miracles happen when the Lord's people walk in obedience to Jesus' teachings. It is very moving to teach new believers Christ's commandment to love one another and to see the Holy Spirit working and transforming their lives, creating new beings loosened from selfishness, thinking of their brothers and sisters, sharing with the less fortunate out of their own poverty.

Let us take the example of Peter. At first, he did not want to receive Christ's blessing. He believed that he was called to serve his master and not to receive from him. He was freed by the sudden realization that he must receive the service of others as well as serve.

The same thing happens in the church when we try to minister to people without letting them minister to us. We have heard and take seriously the strong commandment to be selfless and to give generously, which we have applied even to the issue of inclusiveness in the church. We invite people of other ethnic groups to be part of our fellowship. We provide for the needs of refugees from other countries. We send missionaries, service workers, and fraternal workers all over the world. But we have a hard time being served by people of other cultures.

We have a hard time relinquishing the pulpit on Sunday morning to a person from another culture or learning a song in Spanish or asking newcomers and people of other ethnic groups to be Sunday school teachers and church board members. There is a certain unspoken expectation many times that the foreigner or stranger among us must first conform to be like us. We have stooped to wash another's feet, but, like Peter, we protest when someone wants to wash our feet. We ought to be ready to receive and give and thus know the blessing of obedience and love.

Jesus said to Peter, "Unless I wash you, you have no share with me." Then Peter does a flip-flop and wants only to be served. Jesus tells him it cannot be only one way or the other but must be both: "One who has bathed does not need to wash, except for the feet, but is entirely clean." He urges Peter to keep everything in balance.

The new Hispanic congregation in Santa Ana is an example of the balance between serving and being served. But it is still not a finished work. God continues working daily on both groups. Hispanics and European-Americans are being challenged for service and understanding of each other's culture. The challenge is to be one in Christ in such a way that the community around us can say, "Behold, how they love one another!" ¡Sumos uno en Cristo!

Discussion and Action

1. Share with the group what has impressed you most in your reading and study of this text.
2. According to your understanding, what are the most important points of this Bible lesson (John 13:1-17)?
3. Does your denomination practice feetwashing? What other expressions of mutuality does your church practice? Why do you think it is difficult for churches to receive love and service from others as Jesus commanded? Is it difficult for you to receive service from others?

4. Demonstrate in some special way the meaning of love as given in Jesus' example. For instance, hold a handwashing or feetwashing for your Covenant group.
5. Where have you experienced a two-way ministry—giving and receiving—between people of different cultures? How can your Covenant group practice this mutual love?
6. Decide on some specific action in which you can serve as well as be served. Consider inviting a congregation of another background to have a joint worship, drawing on the resources of both groups.

Olga Serrano

9

In Christ A New Creation
2 Corinthians 5

Paul reminds the church at Corinth, a church struggling with issues that continue to affect the church of Jesus Christ today, to practice reconciliation, calling them back to their mission as the body of Christ.

Personal Preparation

1. Read 2 Corinthians 5. Do you feel you have been reconciled to God? What changes took place in you?
2. Name a cultural problem that seems so hopeless that it cannot be solved.
3. Think of a reconciliation in which you believe God had a hand. Is there someone with whom you would like to be reconciled now? How can you take the initiative to bring about the reconciliation?
4. Name the ways that you represent Jesus' mission every day.

Understanding

The last several years have brought a noticeable increase in the manifestation of tribalism throughout the world. Much of the attitude of people around the world seems to be, *What is important is me and mine. No other group or race has the same rights and privileges as we do. In fact, they do not even have the same right to life and liberty as my group. We can therefore devalue them, dehumanize them, or if we choose, we can eliminate them.* This tribalism is making itself known all over the world. In places as culturally diverse as Eastern Europe and Southern Africa or South Central Los Angeles and New York City, we tend to value people who are most like us.

The problem is not that we place too high a value on our heritage and culture. Such value is a good thing; all of us are strongest when we have a good sense of who we are, based on our cultural ancestry. The problem occurs when we not only value ourselves and our own background but, at the same time, devalue the background or history of those who are different from us. We become so focused on what our particular needs are that others' needs are minimized, oppressed, or threatened with annihilation.

So separated are we in our own society that if we chose we could probably win a divorce from one another on grounds of "irreconcilable differences." Too often, in both church and society, we recognize little common ground. We use the same words, but speak different languages. We find other cultures almost totally incomprehensible to us, and we have little interest in gaining any firsthand information about each other. We are radically and hopelessly separated from one another.

The church is no less guilty of the vast cultural separation than secular society. Churches, which have a particular call and obligation to be agents of healing and hope, have too often become supporters of the culture instead of helpful critics. Like participants at a political convention, groups in the church vie for influence and a voice in church politics. At times we can hardly hear each other for all the shouting. In all the noise, the cries of those who would join the church in mission get lost. It is not an easy time for the church now, and it was not an easy time for Paul and his brother and sister Christians when Second Corinthians was written.

Trust had broken down between Paul and the church at Corinth. We are not sure what caused the breach, but we do know that it was serious enough for Paul to delay a planned visit to the city and to send a letter instead. The letter mentioned in 2 Corinthians 2:3 is lost to us now, but it explained his reasons for not coming to Corinth. He apparently postponed his visit in order to spare himself and the church what he believed would be another painful visit (2:1). By the time he sent the letter that we know as 2 Corinthians, Paul was reconciled with the church. He was reassured that he and the church were not at irreversible odds with each other. Out of that reality Paul can instruct the church on the importance of reconciliation.

Paul reminds the church at Corinth, a church struggling with issues that continue to affect the church of Jesus Christ today (the role of women, the integrity of marriage, human sexuality, the place of the Lord's supper, for example), that Jesus Christ is the center of their lives and mission. Conflict and animosity were devilishly distracting the Corinthians, but Paul calls them back to their mission as the body of Christ.

Paul begins the fifth chapter with a statement of faith. He reminds the Corinthians that their trust in God is so strong that it can be maintained even in the face of death. Having suffered and grown in his own ministry, Paul is qualified to declare that God's help and presence will only increase in strength once this earthly life is past (vv. 1-10).

After Paul establishes the faith of the Corinthians, he moves to the heart of the chapter (vv. 14-20), the lesson on reconciliation. The faithful are changed people. They have been reconciled to God through Jesus, the great reconciler and, as ambassadors of Christ, they also take on the ministry of reconciliation. As God has reconciled the world through Jesus Christ, so the community of faith is to be reconciled to one another and to God.

The ministry of reconciliation of one to another is formed in three ways. First, the ministry is formed by the love of Christ which, according to Paul, "urges us on" (v. 14). It is a love so strong and sacrificial that it was willing to endure the cross on behalf of humanity.

Second, from our vantage point at the foot of the cross and standing at the empty tomb, we have a new insight. We are able to see Jesus as the risen Lord, not as human martyr to a lost cause. It is the new perspective that marks us as being in Christ. Two stories illustrate the point.

The meeting had just begun and while the first item of business was sure to cause some tension, none of the participants could have predicted the strong feelings present around the table. Before the issue was decided, harsh words were spoken, accusations made, and old hurts exposed. One of the people on the losing end of the argument spent the rest of the meeting feeling angry and isolated. Finally, the meeting came to a close with worship and communion. Two of the people who had contended most fiercely at the beginning of the meeting found themselves sitting next to each other. There was still anger between them. But as one passed the bread and cup to the other, they felt a sense of reconciliation between them. Ultimately, they were unable to hear the words of institution and receive the elements of the Lord's Supper and at the same time hold on to anger and frustration. They had to let go of everything that kept them apart. In that moment they were reconciled. Christ the Reconciler had become known to them in the literal breaking of bread.

I was reminded in another incident that with our new perspective we are brought together by Christ Jesus in a way that unites us more than our differences separate us. Cecil Murray, an African Methodist Episcopal pastor, was in the forefront of the news right after the disturbances in Los Angeles in the spring of 1992. Fully aware that some of the anger of the African-American community was aimed at Korean businesses, and knowing that those two communities would have to work together in order for there to be a just and lasting peace in South Central Los Angeles, Murray and some of his parishioners went to worship with a Korean congregation. When Murray and the others arrived, members of the host congregation had already arrived. As their guests entered the sanctuary, the Koreans stood and began singing in Korean "It Is Well with My Soul." There is reconciliation when adversaries can share the eucharist and worship God together.

In addition to the motivations of love and new life in Christ, the ministry of reconciliation of one to another has its source in our reconciliation to God. Paul speaks of himself and those with him as ambassadors for Christ (v. 20). And it is on behalf of the one who sent them that Paul offers one last word of advice: "Be reconciled to God." He is telling the church that all relationships begin out of our right relationships with God.

What do these words mean for a deeply divided, multicultured world? We could easily argue for simply accepting as a reality an unreconciled life, both in terms of our life with God and our life with each other. Popular culture bombards us with the message that we are farther apart than we have ever been before.

The nightly news tells us that, while there may no longer be a cold war, there are dozens of small, international and civil wars being waged many times over cultural dominance. In our own country, we are battling white supremacist groups, police brutality, racism, and discrimination. Films and television programs remind us of the things that make us anxious about each other. Issues of race, sex, and class lie behind much of what separates us.

What then shall we do? Happily, as Christians we do not have to live as if reconciliation is coming. We live in the reality that it is already here! To live as people reconciled to God and to each other is not to live in a naive fantasy. Rather, it is to live knowing the promises of God are true. When we are reconciled to God through Jesus Christ, our human relationships will still be troublesome, but they have the potential of being changed for the better because God has pledged to be with us.

Discussion and Action

1. Think about a time of reconciliation. When did it happen and what were the circumstances that made it possible for reconciliation to take place?
2. Recall a time when reconciliation was not possible. What were the circumstances that prevented reconciliation from taking place?
3. In light of the understanding of reconciliation, recall a time of reconciliation between you and God. Recall also a time when reconciliation between you and God was not possible. Why?
4. Talk about shows you have seen on television that bring out the anxieties between cultures and races. Notice the subtleties in media. Make a list of recent movies and programs about other cultures. In another column list the main character. Note how many times the main character comes from the same culture featured in the film. Why do you think they are the same or different?
5. Is there any controversy in your church or community in which you could be ambassadors of reconciliation? Talk as a group about how you can bring about reconciliation. Covenant to carry out the initiative.
6. How can we be reconcilers to people who are not reconciled to God? What should our attitude be toward people of other faiths with whom we might be at war?

LaTaunya M. Bynum

10

On the Pilgrimage Together
Acts 2

God broke into the world at Pentecost to establish the church, bringing Gentile and Jew together in a new way. But the new church was never perfect. The church still struggles, as it did in the account in Acts, for a unity that values diversity.

Personal Preparation

1. Think back over the lessons in *Many Cultures, One in Christ*. What new insights about cultural diversity do you have? How have you changed the way you think about other cultures in the church?
2. How would a person from a different ethnic background than yours feel if they visited your church?
3. Read Joshua 24. Then read Acts 2. How are the events alike? How are they different?
4. Think of the ethnic diversity in your church. What can your church do to help people live together?

Understanding

On New Year's Day we have seen the traditional picture of spry old Father Time with a long flowing beard, holding a baby in one arm and a sickle in the other, representing the passage of time. Out with the old, in with the new. The old man is actually derived from the Greek god Cronus, who was a god of the harvest. Cronus is usually pictured as an old man, in the harvest years of his life, holding a sickle. From his name we have words such as *chronology* (the order of things) and *chronic* (things that happen at regular intervals). Whether we like it or not, much of life is governed by Father Time. The moments, days, and years plod on. And even though we have a hard time describing what time is, we see its effects in our houses, cars, children, hairlines, and waistlines!

Cronus is not, however, the only timekeeper. Occasionally, time seems not to exist at all. We all have had moments when we say that time stood still or time seemed like an eternity or time seemed to fly by. The Greek term for the moments when time is suspended and God is in our presence is *kairos*. For instance, sealing a covenant with God that changes everything, that interrupts business as usual to start something new, is a *kairos* moment.

We began this study with a kairos moment, the momentous covenant at Shechem, an event that changed the world (Josh. 24:1-28). A covenant is an agreement for change. It joins a solitary man and a solitary woman into a union that is more than the two individuals put together. A covenant unites a single believer to a believing community, and both the believer and the community are changed. The covenant at Shechem brought people together in Canaan who were originally from Egypt, Canaan, Syria, and Mesopotamia. They came together to form a new group with a revolutionary vision for the future. Covenant-making is a thing that changes the course of time and all of life.

Kairos moments, such as the sealing of the covenant, give us a taste of the world that we anticipate with the fullness of the reign of God. They are blissful moments when we can say this must be what the kingdom is like. We celebrate the meaning of those moments in history and look forward to more such moments, but at the same time we know that we can never fully embody complete perfection this side of the fullness of God's reign. While we live with our sights on the vision of a harmonious multicultural world, the reality of racism (Matt. 15:21-28) characterizes life in chronos time.

The Pentecost in Acts 2 is another kairos moment when something brand new happens to change the world. God breaks into chronological time and suspends it for a moment to give us a vision. The vision does not obliterate all the problems of the world. It gives us a goal toward which to work, the promise of Acts.

The first verse of Acts 2 provides two ingredients for a story of kairos: a gathering of people and a special event. People are gathered for Pentecost, which means "fiftieth" in Greek. This name marked the celebration of the Jewish Feast of Weeks. Like the Thanksgiving holiday in the United States and Canada, Pentecost is an agricultural celebration for the good that God has bestowed on the community. Over time, Pentecost came to be a thanksgiving for God's acts in history as well as for agricultural bounty. Pentecost is a time for people to come together in an attitude of gratitude.

At this typical annual festival where many people were assembled, the whole atmosphere suddenly changed with the inbreaking of God's spirit. The wind blew and fire surrounded them. Surely a change in wind and weather or the onset of fire was not new to the people there. So what was so new that day? The Holy Spirit did not merely send the wind and the fire. The Holy Spirit *was* the wind and the fire, and that was new!

God's presence in some earthly form for all to see, such as this, is called a theophany. The tongues of fire remind us of other theophanies where God is represented as fire. In some theophanies, such as the burning bush, God appears to impart knowledge. The image of God as fire has also served as protection and guidance as in the pillar of cloud and pillar of fire (Exod. 13:21-22; 19:9; 33:9; 40:34-38; 1 Kgs. 8:10-11). In Acts, fire and wind represent God as a God of justice, treating all equally just as the wind blows over everyone and fire consumes everything in its path without discrimination. The use of "tongues" to describe the fire expands the vision of a God of justice, for tongues are also languages that represent the variety of people in the world. The expression "tongues of fire" is a play on words that indicates God comes to everyone of every tongue.

Often we rush past the emphasis on equality in the passage. Acts 2 indicates that the Holy Spirit does not discriminate between people as the world does or as even the church does. As we have seen earlier, those far off (those who were kept out of the tight circle of the faithful) are now brought near. As Paul says: "So then you are no longer strangers and aliens, but you are citizens with the saints and also members of the household of God" (Eph. 2:19). Everyone present received the Holy Spirit, the insider and the outsider.

The church has been responsible for keeping many people "far off." As immigrants to North America, many of us arrived with an ethnic identity that was wedded to a religious identity through particular denominations. Even today, we are tempted to mix up our ethnic identity with our religious identity. We have ascribed religious characteristics to ethnic ones, such as dress, frugality, "simple living," and even certain types of foods. Denominations can become specially designed ethnic ghettos for those hoping to hold on to ethnic identity through the vehicle of the church.

Even the hymns we love from our childhood in racially and culturally homogeneous congregations reflect our desire to live in a past that was exclusive. Some of us believe, for instance, that old favorite gospel hymns are the only truly sacred music and all other hymns are merely songs. How would we feel at a worship service that used African-American sacred music exclusively, except for a few German hymns sung during German History Month?

Picture the congregation that had a monthly potluck after church. One Sunday a family who had recently returned from a year in Japan brought some seaweed cakes and sushi. Many of the people at the potluck did not find these dishes tasty in the least. What, if any, is the proper religious food? What should people bring to the church potluck? What is religious and what is cultural?

Or consider the evangelical church that invited an apostolic congregation to worship with them one Sunday to promote friendship and understanding. To open the worship, the apostolic members passed out a confession of faith and asked everyone to read it in unison. Many in the host church grumbled quietly as they read over the sheet, feeling they were about to be forced to utter words they did not exactly accept. What are the proper words? Does God hear all expressions of faith or just ours? What is merely a cultural outlook and what is the true confession?

Look at the Sunday school teacher who wanted to teach children in Sunday school how others see God. When she had students draw pictures of God as a bear (Lam. 3:10), a mother hen (Matt. 23:37), a burning bush (Exod. 3:2), and the wind (Acts 2:2), there was an uproar in the church. Over hundreds of years, the church universal has settled on the image of God as a person like us, but the Bible uses many nonhuman images to describe God. Is there a single proper way to talk about God?

Not all of those who were present at the Pentecost became witnesses for Jesus Christ. Some were bewildered by the strange thing that happened. As Jews they knew the story of the tower of Babel in Genesis 11, which explained why there were many languages in the world. According to the story, the world began with one language. The people of the world sought to use the common language and technology to build a ladder to heaven (11:1-4), but God saw the potential for trouble, knowing that people were always seeking power. While the people plotted a way to consolidate their power, God was at work to prevent it. God diversified and dispersed the people to avoid disaster.

The message of the Pentecost that some failed to hear and we fail to grasp even today is that God still favors diversity, because no single person or group has the authority to value one expression of faith over another. The more expressions, the better. But Acts is the story of one problem after another between Gentiles and Jews, mostly over cultural practices. Did the new church fail to accomplish the unity that God desired, the unity of the covenant at Shechem? No. Diversity has its problems, but uniformity is impossible and undesirable. A single style, a uniform way of worship, one language, one orthodox belief is too puny for God. That we can all speak a different language but still understand each other is very hard and very good indeed!

Discussion and Action

1. Think back over the lessons in *Many Cultures, One in Christ*. Share with the group any new insights about cultural diversity that you have. Tell how you have changed the way you think about other cultures in the church.
2. Come up with a rough plan to make your worship more inviting to people of other cultures. See that it is carried out.
3. What parts of the text struck you this week? How did the young church change and grow and struggle for unity?
4. How are we an extension of the Pentecost? What are our struggles?
5. What other "cultures," such as academic, industrial, economic, agricultural, white collar, social, or theological, exist in your congregation? Are these "cultures" open to everybody, or do they exclude some people? What are the unspoken requirements for belonging? How does it feel to be left out?
6. Tell stories of unity amid diversity out of your church's life.

Stephen Breck Reid

Suggestions for Sharing and Prayer

This material is designed for Covenant Bible study groups who spend time sharing and praying together, followed by a time of Bible study. The ideas and resources offered here will relate the group's sharing and worship life to their study of *Many Cultures, One In Christ*. Groups are encouraged to use those suggestions that fit best with each session and with their own needs; participants may also offer their own unique ideas for the sharing and worship time. This guide was compiled by Harriet Finney, People of the Covenant planning team member, and June Adams Gibble, People of the Covenant coordinator and Church of the Brethren staff person.

Prayers and Praying

❑ Discover some of the many different ways, different postures, and different settings for prayer that are found in the Scriptures. Read the following texts, and look for others. How can these ways of praying enrich our prayer life today?

1 Samuel 1:9-18
Hannah prays silently, in deep distress.

2 Kings 4:32-35
Elisha prays with his actions.

Psalm 55:16-17
The psalmist complains and moans in prayer.

Daniel 6:10-11
Daniel prays three times a day, facing Jerusalem.

Matthew 6:5-13
Pray in secret; the Lord's prayer.

Matthew 26:36-46
Jesus prays in Gethsemane.

Luke 6:12-13
Jesus prays all night before calling disciples.

Luke 18:10-13
The Pharisee and tax collector pray.

John 17
Jesus prays a prayer for his disciples.

Acts 7:59-60
Stephen prays before death.

1 Thessalonians 5:16-18
Pray without ceasing.

Romans 8:26-27
The Spirit intercedes when we don't know how to pray.

❑ Pray for the different peoples and countries of the world that
have been in the news this week. Begin your prayers with
words such as: "O God, our Creator, our Redeemer, sustain
the people of . . . " or "Dear God, there are places in this
world we will never visit and people we will never meet, but
we know they are there, and you know about them . . . "

❑ Use prayers from different cultures, countries, and
peoples—prayers that call you to be aware of global issues
and concerns.

❑ Individually, or as a group discipline, use the book *A World
at Prayer: The New Ecumenical Prayer Cycle* (see p. xii).
Pray for different areas of the world each week. Here are
several prayers from this rich resource:

Lord, you have the whole wide world in your hands;
You are able to turn human hearts as seems best to you;
grant your grace therefore to the bonds of peace and love,
and in all lands join together whatever has been torn asunder.

(Evangelical Church of the River Plate,
Argentina. Used by permission.)

O God of many names
Lover of all nations
We pray for peace
in our hearts
in our homes
in our nations
in our world
the peace of your will
the peace of our need.

(Week of Prayer for World Peace.
Used by permission.)

Sacred Art

❏ Look for artwork that portrays Jesus and other biblical
   characters as people from different cultural/ethnic
   perspectives. Check in bookstores, public libraries, and
   church libraries for pictures, prints, and art books, such as
   *Christ and the Fine Arts, The Old Testament and the Fine
   Arts,* and *Great Madonnas of the World.*

❏ Visit other church buildings, retreat centers, or cathedrals in
   your community to see how artists have portrayed Jesus and
   Bible stories in stained glass, statuary, and paintings.

Building Relationships

❏ Challenge your group to meet, learn to know, share and work
   with people whose cultural and ethnic identity are different
   from your own. Even if you think your community is not
   multicultural, look for opportunities. For example, one
   midwestern congregation, located in an almost all-white
   community, shares their baptistery with a pentecostal
   Hispanic congregation.

❏ Call your denominational headquarters and ask to be put in
   touch with a "sister congregation" whose members come
   from a different culture or ethnicity; contact them by phone
   or letter and decide on ways you would like to relate.

❏ Invite someone to meet with your group and tell about their
   trip to another country or a visit in a different ethnic
   community. This could be from business travel, a work camp
   experience, volunteer service work, mission work, or an
   exchange student program. Or encourage a member of your
   group to participate in a work camp, to work on a disaster
   response team, or to worship with another congregation.
   Then have them share this experience.

Foods and Eating Together

❏ Invite each person in your group to share foods from his or
   her own cultural or ethnic background, either sharing a
   different food and tradition each week or having one large
   smorgasbord.

❑ Invite people from another church in your community that predominantly represents a different culture/race/ethnicity than your own, to share with you in a carry-in meal and worship time. Ask the other group to contribute foods and worship resources from their tradition.

Film and Video

❑ Learn more about the culture of different ethnic groups in your community or your denomination by watching a film in the other language, using the subtitles to follow the story, or by viewing travel films, often available from public libraries. Talk about how it feels to not understand fully what's going on.

❑ Do further study on prejudice, racism, and discriminatory attitudes and actions that permeate our culture and affect life today. View the video "True Colors," from ABC's program "Prime Time," which follows two men—one white, one black—through a variety of everyday situations (including renting an apartment, seeking a job, buying a car). [$10.00 rental from Brethren Press (1-800-441-3712) or Brethren Audio-Visual Library (1-717-545-2916)]

Music and Singing

❑ Enjoy music from various cultures, bringing cassette tapes and records for your group to listen to together. Learn to sing along with some of the music.

❑ Go through your denominational hymnal(s) and look for hymns in different languages. How many different selections do you find? What languages are represented? Identify the country/nationality of the musicians and the text writers.

❑ Find hymns with words that talk about the gift of diversity and the unity possible in Christ in the midst of diversity. A good example is "In Christ There Is No East or West." Some hymnals have this hymn in different languages. Sing some of these hymns, or use the words as prayer, responsive reading, or small group meditations.

❑ Name some of the spirituals that have given meaning to your faith, such as: "Were You There When They Crucified My

Lord?"; "Steal Away, Steal Away, Steal Away to Jesus";
"Swing Low, Sweet Chariot"; "Lord, I Want to Be a
Christian"; "Let Us Break Bread Together." Sing some of
your favorites. Look for other African-American hymns or
music that is new to you; if possible, learn some of them.

❑ Sing hymns in different languages, perhaps inviting people
from your congregation or the wider community to teach you
these hymns. Two possibilities follow:

Jesus Loves Me

English:

> Jesus loves me! this I know,
> for the Bible tells me so.
> Little ones to him belong,
> they are weak, but he is strong.
> Yes, Jesus loves me. Yes, Jesus loves me.
> Yes, Jesus loves me, the Bible tells me so.

Spanish:

> Cristo me ama, me ama a mi.
> Su palabra dice así.
> Niños pueden ir a El,
> quien es nuestro Amigo fiel.
> Sí, Cristo me ama. Sí, Cristo me ama.
> Sí, Cristo me ama, la Biblia dice así.

Korean:

> Yesu sarang Hasiman
> Georukhasin marilsei
> Wooridrn Yakana
> Yesu gwonsei mantoda.
> Nal sarang hasim. Nal sarang hasim.
> Nal sarang hasim, Seong gyongei sseoitne.

What a Friend We Have in Jesus

English:

> What a friend we have in Jesus,
>> all our sins and griefs to bear!
> What a privilege to carry everything to God in prayer!
> Oh, what peace we often forfeit,
>> oh, what needless pain we bear,
> All because we do not carry everything to God in prayer.

Spanish:

> ¡Oh qué amigo nos es Cristo! El llevó nuestro dolor,
> y nos manda que llevemos todo a Dios en oración.
> ¿Vive el hombre desprovisto de paz, gozo y santo amor?
> Esto es porque no llevamos todo a Dios en oración.

Korean:

> Joejm matteun uri goojoo, otji jo-eun chingooji
> Georjeong geunsim moogeounjim uri jookke makkise.
> Jookke goham om neun go ro bokeul batji mottane
> Saramdri otjikayeo aroeljurul marulga.
>> Sikeom gugjeong modeun geogrom.

Ways of Worshiping God

❑ Think of the variety of ways that people in Scripture worship God. Check these texts and find others. Talk about the many different ways congregations and people worship God today.

Exodus 15:20-21
Miriam's song of thanks, with dancing and tambourine

Isaiah 58:5-7
The fasting and worship that God chooses

Psalm 150
Praise God with instrument and dance

Micah 6:6-8
How shall I come before God?

Amos 5:21-24
True worship means justice and righteousness

Ephesians 5:18b-20
Filled with the Spirit, singing, giving thanks

General Worship Resources

❑ Call to Celebration

> We are family . . . the family of God!
> Let us celebrate this marvelous identity.
> For abundant life cannot be found alone, but only in community:
> community that reaches, invites, and includes all people, even me.
> Come, let us worship the God who shapes us,
> making many people one people,
> through Jesus Christ, our Lord.

(By John W. Lowe, Jr.)

❑ Invocation

Come to Us, O God
English:

> Come to us, O God!
> Come as wind and inspire;
> Come as fire and empower;
> Come as dove and bring us peace;
> Come as water and cleanse our hearts;
> So that we may know your presence and
> Walk more closely to you. Amen.

Spanish:

> Miranos ¡Oh Dios!
> Ven como el viento e inspira
> Ven como el fuego y fortalece
> Ven como la paloma y traenos la Paz
> Ven como el agua y limpia mi ser
> Envia tu Aliento para que podamos caminar junto a ti
> Y sentir tu maravillosa presencia. ¡Atencion!

Korean:

오 하나님 ! 우리에게 오소서 !
바람처럼 오셔서, 우리를 감동케 하시고,
불길처럼 오셔서, 능력으로 옷입혀 주소서.
비둘기처럼 오셔서, 우리를 평화케 하소서.
빗물처럼 오셔서, 우리의 마음을 깨끗케 하소서.
주의 성령을 보내주셔서, 우리로 주님께 더욱 가까히 가게 하시고
주께서 우리와 함께 하시는 기적을 우리로 깨닫게 하소서 !
아멘.

(By Carol Bowman Gnagy, from
For All Who Minister, © 1993, Brethren Press)

□ Affirmations of Faith

From a wandering nomad, you created your family;
for a burdened people, you raised up a leader;
for a confused nation, you chose a king;
for a rebellious crowd, you sent your prophets.
In these last days, you have sent us your Son,
your perfect image, bringing your kingdom,
revealing your will, dying, rising, reigning,
remaking your people for yourself.

(Church of the Province of Kenya, from
A World at Prayer. Used by permission.)

We believe in God who loves us and wants us to love
each other.
   This is our God.
We believe in Jesus who cared about children and held
them in his arms. He wanted a world where everyone
could live together in peace.
   This is Jesus Christ.
We believe in the Holy Spirit who keeps working with us
until everything is good and true.
   This is the Holy Spirit.

We can be the Church which reminds people of God
because we love each other.
This we believe. Amen.

(From children's worship, WCC Seventh Assembly,
Canberra, Australia, 1991. Used by permission.)

❑ Prayers

O God, you are like a weaver-woman in our lives. Out of
the energy of the universe you have spun each one of us
into a unique, colorful strand with our own special hue
and texture, and have woven us together into your human
family that blankets the globe. We admit that our own
choices have severed us from your loom of life and
created rents in the whole of our human fabric.

We have allowed ourselves to be bound by the narrow
contexts into which we were born and now live our daily
lives. . . . We have often refused to ask the hard questions
that need to be asked for the sake of the well-being of all
people.

O weaver-woman God, open our eyes to the mystery and
power of your Spirit. Refresh us with the light of your
vision so that we may once again recognize the beauty
and wonder of the specially spun thread that we are, the
splendor of the one colorful cloth of humanity. Reattach
us to your loom so that your vision may be made plain
through us.

In the name of the Christ, the One who was at one with all
of life. Amen.

(USA, from *A World at Prayer.* Used by permission.)

Great God, we meet you in many images:
   A mother who comforts her child,
   A father kind to his children,
   A child who leads us,
   A friend who cares,
   A husband, a wife—loving and faithful,
   Someone from another culture,
   Someone who lifts our burden,

A stranger, prisoner, sick one we serve,
All who share faith, service, worship with us.

Accept our thanks that you have not created us solitary beings. Unite us in the wider family of humankind as sisters and brothers in Jesus Christ. Amen.

(By Samuel H. Flora, Jr., from
For All Who Minister, © 1993, Brethren Press)

❏ A Litany for Christian Unity

"How very good and pleasant it is when kindred live together in unity! It is like the precious oil on the head, running down . . . on the beard of Aaron, . . . over the collar of his robes." (Psa. 133:1-2)

O God, pour upon us the precious oil of unity, that we may move forward with one mind and one spirit. Give us courage enough to be honest about our differences and grace enough to accept each other as you accept us.

"I ask not only on behalf of these, but also on behalf of those who will believe in me through their word, that they may all be one." (John 17:20-21a)

Our God, to whom Jesus prayed, may the prayer of our Lord be fulfilled. Draw us closer to all who name the name of Christ, that the world may know the saving power of your love.

"There is one body and one Spirit . . . one hope, . . . one Lord, one faith, one baptism, one God and Father of all, who is above all and through all and in all." (Eph. 4:4-6)

Though many in our understandings of your truth, O God, we are of one body and one spirit with Christians of every time and place. Lift our vision beyond these walls, beyond the boundaries of town, state, and nation. Help us to see the face of Christ in the faces of others. Fill us with passion to give of ourselves for his sake and for the world Christ came to save. Amen.

(By Kenneth L. Gibble)

❑ Benedictions

> Go now and be aware that Jesus overcame the walls
> which separated Jew and Gentile, owner and slave, men
> and women. Go now and proclaim to the world that the
> walls have fallen:
>
> > —no more shall we allow wealth to keep us from
> > identifying with the poor;
> > —no more shall anyone convince us that as human
> > beings we don't even know are our enemies;
> > —no more shall skin color or sex make one person feel
> > inferior to another.
>
> Be reconciled as one in Christ. Embrace as sisters and
> brothers.
> Go now in peace.
>
> > (By Ingrid Rogers, from *Women at the Well.* © 1987,
> > Womaen's Caucus of the Church of the Brethren.
> > Used with permission.)

> May God bless and keep you.
> May the very face of God shine on you
> > and be gracious to you.
> May God's presence embrace you
> > and give you peace.
>
> > (© 1992, The Hymnal Project)

> Go in love,
> > for love alone endures.
> Go in peace,
> > for it is the gift of God.
> Go in safety,
> > for we cannot go where God is not.
>
> > (By Earle W. Fike, Jr., from *Hymnal:
> > A Worship Book*, © 1992.)

Jubilate Deo omnis terra

*Translation: Rejoice in the Lord, all lands. Serve the Lord with gladness. Alleluia!

Text: based on Psalm 100
Music: Jacques Berthier, 1980

Jesu, Jesu, Fill Us with Your Love

REFRAIN

Je - su, Je - su, fill us with your love, show
us how to serve the neigh - bors we have from you.

Fine

1. Kneels at the feet of his friends, si - lent ly wash - es their
2. Neigh - bors are rich and poor, neigh - bors are black, brown and
3. These are the ones we should serve, these are the ones we should
4. Lov - ing puts us on our knees, serv - ing as though we are
5. Kneel at the feet of our friends, si - lent - ly wash - ing their

D. C.

feet, Mas - ter who acts as a slave to them.
white, neigh - bors are near - by and far a - way.
love, all these are neigh - bors to us and you.
slaves, this is the way we should live with you.
feet, this is the way we should live with you.

Text: Tom Colvin, 1969
Music: Ghana Folk Song; adapted by Tom Colvin, 1969; arr. by Jane Marshall, 1982

Will you let me be your servant

1,6 Will you let me be your ser - vant, let me
2 We are pil - grims on a jour - ney, we are
3 I will hold the Christ - light for you in the
4 I will weep when you are weep - ing, when you
5 When we sing to God in heav - en, we shall

1,6 be as Christ to you? Pray that I may have the
2 trav - 'lers on the road. We are here to help each
3 night - time of your fear. I will hold my hand out
4 laugh I'll laugh with you. I will share your joy and
5 find such har - mon - y, born of all we've known to -

1,6 grace to let you be my ser - vant too.
2 oth - er walk the mile and bear the load.
3 to you, speak the peace you long to hear.
4 sor - row till we've seen this jour - ney through.
5 geth - er of Christ's love and a - gon - y.

*Guitar chords for unison singing only.

Text: Richard Gillard, 1977, alt.
Music: Richard Gillard, 1977; adapted by Betty Pulkingham
    Text and Music copyright © 1977 Scripture in Song

Other Covenant Bible Studies available from *faithQuest:*